W9-BVA-903

A12█████448479

More Advance Praise for *The Mid-Career Tune-Up*

"*The Mid-Career Tune-Up* is more than a book; it's an interactive guide that can help anyone create an intensely personal and meaningful blueprint for successfully coping with today's faster, technology-based workplace."

WITHDRAWN

—Nate Rosenblatt, President,
NPR Marketing, Inc.

"Salmon and Salmon have written a very complete, practical guide to managing your career smartly. Especially transitioning into the new millennium, we all could benefit from this mid-career tune-up."

—Dr. Katherine N. Huston, Senior Partner,
Organization Resources Group;
Adjunct Professor in Organizational Management,
Cabrini College

"This book is filled with pragmatic, practical, and proven techniques for making the most of your work life. A great resource for anyone who wishes to "tune-up" their career—middle, early, or late."

—Dana Robinson, President, Partners in Change, Inc.;
co-author of *Performance Consulting*

"The Salmons have offered practical advice and hands-on tools for taking control of your career and improving your skills and attitudes."

—Marianne S. Gauss, Assistant Professor,
La Salle University

"Want to know what you and your career will REALLY be facing in the next century? This little book provides not only spot-on insight but uncompromising straight talk on the skills we'll all need to keep pace and flourish."

—Orlando R. Barone, President,
Barone Associates Management Consultants

The Mid-Career Tune-Up

10 New Habits for Keeping Your Edge in Today's Fast-Paced Workplace

William A. Salmon
and
Rosemary T. Salmon

I.C.C. LIBRARY

AMACOM
American Management Association
New York · Atlanta · Boston · Chicago · Kansas City · San Francisco · Washington, D.C.
Brussels · Mexico City · Tokyo · Toronto

HF
5381
.S256
2000

Special discounts on bulk quantities of AMACOM books are available to corporations, professional associations, and other organizations. For details, contact Special Sales Department, AMACOM, an imprint of AMA Publications, a division of American Management Association, 1601 Broadway, New York, NY 10019. Tel.: 212-903-8316. Fax: 212-903-8083.

This publication is designed to provide accurate and authoritative information in regard to the subject matter covered. It is sold with the understanding that the publisher is not engaged in rendering legal, accounting, or other professional service. If legal advice or other expert assistance is required, the services of a competent professional person should be sought.

Library of Congress Cataloging-in-Publication Data

Salmon, William A.

The mid-career tune-up : 10 new habits for keeping your edge in today's fast-paced workplace / William A. Salmon and Rosemary T. Salmon.

p. cm.

Includes index.

ISBN 0-8144-0523-1

1. Career development. 2. Success in business. 3. Job satisfaction. 4. Job security. I. Salmon, Rosemary. II. Title.

HF5381.S256 1999

650.14—dc21   *99–40033*

                                           CIP

© 2000 William A. Salmon and Rosemary T. Salmon.
All rights reserved.
Printed in the United States of America.

This publication may not be reproduced, stored in a retrieval system, or transmitted in whole or in part, in an form or by any means, electronic, mechanical, photocopying, recording, or otherwise, without the prior written permission of AMACOM, an imprint of AMA Publications, a division of American Management Association, 1601 Broadway, New York, NY 10019.

Printing number

10 9 8 7 6 5 4 3 2

To **Rosemary:**
Everything I am, I am for you
—**Bill**

To **Bill,** my hero:
His life was gentle; and the elements so mixt in him,
that Nature might stand up and say to all the world,
"This was a Man!" *William Shakespeare*
—**Rosemary**

Contents

Acknowledgments

Before this book reached publication stage, my husband, Bill, passed away. Our five children helped us both through the final chapter in the last month of Bill's life. I am forever indebted to them for their love and their organizational skills, which helped me prepare this book for final submission. Their dad would be proud.

I am also indebted to Barbara and Bart Frederick, kind neighbors and former school teachers, who stepped in and saved the day by proofreading the copy for us when Bill got too ill to work. To Mike Sivilli, our Associate Editor at AMACOM: a special thanks for beyond-duty patience and sensitivity. And to Jacquie Flynn at AMACOM, for her feedback and suggestions.

Bill had asked me to acknowledge the help given to us and express our thanks to the following special people: Our literary agent Sheree Bykofsky, for her never-wavering confidence in us. Karen DiNunzio, Cynthia Federico, Rob Hartwell, Tina Hartwell, Steve Kauffman, Celestine Mack, Dorothy Meyers, Chris Rose, Elena Rubiales, Siuberto Socarras, and Sue Strong, for their valuable insights. Steve Ozer, for his ongoing support and help with our writing efforts. And Bill's father, John Salmon, for his life-long inspiration to both of us.

Introduction

New Work Habits for Keeping Your Edge in Today's Fast-Paced Workplace

Let us stop equating work with earning a living, but rather think of it as an important component of making a life.

—Ralph C. Weinrich, *Michigan Business Review*

As we move rapidly into a new century, there is no question that competitive economic pressures and changing organizational structures are having a dramatic impact on the American workforce. The pace of work has accelerated, and there is a greater need than ever before for workers to understand priorities, manage their time, and produce high-quality results. The scope of work has expanded, and individual employees are now being challenged to collaborate with others in making decisions, solving problems, and resolving conflicts. The nature of work has changed drastically, and performance expectations are now based on new competencies like accountability, flexibility, and continuous improvement. To survive and succeed in this dynamic, highly competitive atmosphere, American companies and their employees must develop new work habits and discover new ways to apply traditional skills.

To survive and succeed in today's fast-paced workplaces, we may have to change some of our fundamental perspectives about the nature and value of what we do every day. For many of us, our earliest impressions of work were handed down to us from parents and grandparents who lived through the Depression and World War II and clung to the worst of jobs in order to survive. Raised with their unwavering work ethic ("Stop complaining, at least you have a job!"), the majority of us grew up facing the prospect of work with a certain lack of confidence and a limited amount of enthusiasm. Having a job, any job, became and has remained a top priority. Many people, in fact, have learned that so much depends on their ability to get and keep a job that they are willing to glorify their modest accomplishments just to get an entry-level position. They often tolerate an employer's unrealistic demands, lower their expectations, and occasionally even accept positions that neither challenge nor interest them. Often it seems that the American worker has adopted a pragmatic credo—"It's not exactly the job I wanted; but after all, it is a job." This type of foot-in-the-door success story provides at least some economic security, gives us the right to mingle with other productive members of society, often helps us establish our social identities, and offers us a way to measure our self-worth.

Once we are employed, we often define ourselves by our jobs. Perhaps this custom is a throwback to feudal days when a person's status could be measured quickly by a title or by the name of the estate on which he/she worked. We have taken this practice to a complicated extreme. For example, I recall meeting a complete stranger recently who greeted me with something like: "Hi, I'm Roger McMillan, the assistant regional sales manager of the Middle Atlantic Division, New Product Development Unit, Apex Products and Services." By the time Roger had presented his title credits, I had forgotten his name.

Think about how often we talk about our jobs and how often we identify the importance of people by what they do for a living. Ask someone, "How's the family?" and you might get a fairly typical litany of job duties, titles, and responsibilities: "Well, Joe finished law school in June and joined Hudson, Hudson, Mitchell, and what's-his-name right after graduation. Mary is a dental hygienist. She works for three dentists, but the patients make appointments directly with her to have their teeth cleaned. Patty is a commercial artist for a large advertising agency in Detroit. She made more money last year than I expect to make in the next three years. Now that the kids have all left the nest, Peggy has gone back to work, too. She's only a clerk at a local department store, but she had to start somewhere. Besides, there are good promotion possibilities, and with her previous experience as a bank teller, it won't be long before she becomes a cashier or maybe even an assistant manager."

Poor Peggy! Title competition can be tough—especially in a society that is still reluctant to give equal status to other jobs like parent, PTA president, church volunteer, and teacher's aide. Whether our perceptions are correct or not, we do measure people by the importance we attach to their jobs. Titles provide an easy way to assess associates and highlight our own accomplishments. More importantly, though, a job title tells the world that its owner works for a living. No freeloading here! Time is spent producing something, providing a service, performing a task—for money. Our paychecks identify us as active members of the American working population.

Sixty years ago our parents and grandparents struggled to keep their membership in that endangered group. Their survival instincts compelled most of us to follow their direction and join a workforce that, during the 1950s and 1960s, became the most productive in the history of the world. Despite the political and social upheavals that shook our country, culture, and institutions during the turbulent 1970s and 1980s, there was still a sense of "business as usual" that kept American companies comfortably ahead of the rest of the world. Those days are gone, and American business is struggling to contend with global competition, a decline in productivity, and pressure to restructure the way work gets done. These and other challenges are unparalleled in our history.

Trying to determine who is to blame for the current problems in corporate offices is a waste of time and energy. Some managers point fingers at employees and say they seem less motivated than ever to provide a fair day's work for higher and higher salaries. Some employees point out management failures and accuse their employers of creating environments in which quality work goes unnoticed and unrewarded. Rather than encourage what could be endless faultfinding and name-calling, we should recognize the role all of us can play in helping our companies improve productivity, deliver quality products and services to customers, and achieve the necessary bottom-line results to remain competitive and prosperous.

Chris Rose, work control manager at Vermont Yankee Nuclear Power Corporation, believes the biggest challenge facing people at work today is the pace of change:

> There are simply more things to do and less time to do them. We can anticipate more change in the next five years than in the last fifty years. The challenge for me is to manage my time carefully, to schedule priorities thoughtfully, and to make sure I maintain balance in my life by safeguarding time with my family. Some people are resistant to change. They give up too easily or refuse to align with others on important work items. They have what I call an "I'm here for the beer" attitude.

In some cases, these unmotivated individuals show up but do as little work as possible. They mistake attendance for active participation; they equate minimal work output with productive performance. Sometimes they are simply warm bodies taking up valuable space in what has become a hectic, fast-paced environment in which teamwork is critical. Often these individuals are filling job slots, but they are barely fulfilling even the most basic requirements and duties of their jobs. Their lack of contribution to team and corporate objectives has an impact on everyone else. There are a number of reasons why people fall into these bad habits and attitudes. They may be overwhelmed by the changes going on around them. They may have decided that they never signed up for the work they are being asked to do today. They may be simply clocking time until they are able to move into a different work or life situation. Whatever the causes, the amount and speed of change is often at the root of the problem.

The world we work in has undergone major changes during our lifetime. Our perceptions, values, and needs are different from those of our parents. The social, political, and economic climate of our country has changed almost as frequently as the seasons. We are bombarded daily with catastrophic news events brought right into our living rooms in vivid, full-colored detail by the mass media.

Unable to deal effectively with the whirlwind pace of life, many people attempt to build protective shells around themselves to cope with turmoil. In fact, coping has become a way of life, a strategy (with companion skills) that anyone can learn conveniently at countless weekend workshops. There is something peacefully passive about coping, and it is certainly more attractive than the active, negative alternative we once called "copping out." Both options, however, point out a growing sense of helplessness, a feeling of futility and inability to control our own destinies.

Some individuals perceive themselves as victims and act accordingly, banding together in huddled lunch-time groups searching for someone to guide, protect, and lead them. Self-reliance is a thing of the past. In many cases, we have made ourselves dependent on others who cannot possibly have as much at stake in our lives as we do.

This dependency is often most apparent at work, and there is a basic contradiction in the way we approach our daily routines. In lunchroom forums, for example, we can be outspoken and assertive about our jobs. But for the rest of the day, we delegate the responsibility of our care to well-meaning, beleaguered managers who try to balance employees' needs with organizational goals and who often resolve new problems with old solutions. Somehow we have become more dependent on others to tell us how we should feel and to define our personal goals. Agents or stewards negotiate our needs. We work for such-and-such a company, never for ourselves. A second, third, or fourth opinion is necessary before we can feel comfortable with our own first decisions. And sometimes, like Dorothy, we attach ourselves to temporary advisers (scarecrows, tinmen, and cowardly lions) and stumble onward toward greater disillusionment (a power-crazed Wizard of Oz).

We depend on rules and regulations designed to provide safety, security, and comfort to the majority of people they are written to protect. We search for a single voice of authority that can bring order to a chaotic situation. All of us admire effective leadership and hope to find managers who will treat us with respect. But if our jobs continue to frustrate and disappoint us, we tend to choose one of three options (described originally by Hugo Barucco in a 1981 *Management Review* article) as our way of responding to work crises:

1. *Fight.* Before we exercise this option, we usually seek help from any number of designated representatives or try to create support for ourselves among our coworkers. Frequently, gathering backers and promoting our own cause takes up most of our time. Energy that could be used in healthy conversations and productive confrontations is often wasted in gripe sessions or grievance disputes in which we take little direct responsibility for resolving the problem or addressing the cause of our disappointment. We can even convince ourselves that such a flurry of activity is our way of fighting the system, or City Hall, as the saying goes.

Sometimes this is a dangerous, almost self-destructive approach. Even people with years of valuable, exemplary performance run the risk of going too far and losing what it has taken them so long to establish. This is what happened to Roger M., an engineer in a large company. In his twenty-five years with the company, he thought he had seen everything. But some of these new changes sounded ridiculous; "change for change sake" is what he calls them. Roger is getting bitter about how these demands are affecting his work. He is critical of what is going on, and he complains about every minor inconvenience or problem. Everything that goes wrong is the company's fault, and Roger is spreading doom and gloom with his coworkers every chance he gets.

Despite his negative attitude, Roger has managed to maintain his usual high level of performance. He does not see any real harm in the venting he is doing. In fact, he has gathered a small following of coworkers who agree with his views and often ask him to present some of their ideas to their manager. During one of these conversations, Roger's manager presented a different version of this completely unacceptable situation by describing the impact Roger's behavior is having on the rest of the work team. Productivity has declined, morale is lower than it has been in years, there are more unresolved conflicts, problems are minimized or ignored, and quality has become a negotiable commodity. Roger's manager made it clear that he depended on this good, veteran employee to set a positive example for the rest of the team and that the complaining had to stop. One of the final outcomes of this meeting was an agreement that Roger would bring any problem and at least one possible solution to his manager before he went to anyone else. In the end, Roger realized how lucky he was that his manager had taken the time to address this problem. Some companies and their managers may not be willing to work with outspoken employees who stir up trouble. Sometimes, valuable, talented employees are simply asked to leave.

2. *Flight.* We leave the disappointing job and try to find a better one somewhere else. Because of current job market conditions, getting another job may not be as difficult as it was in the recent past. It all depends on what we are willing to accept or settle for. Finding an ideal position may take more time and patience than we have. So this alternative usually involves a compromise. We lower our expectations to get any new job we can, or we accept offers from other companies that include unwanted additional pressures for higher pay. Anything, just to escape a situation that is no longer tolerable.

This is the approach Kevin B. decided to take when his company began a major reorganization. Although he was a fifteen-year veteran employee and had survived several other major changes in the way his company operates, Kevin realized that he had lost his confidence and doubted that he had the necessary skills to succeed. As new policies, procedures, and approaches were announced, Kevin became more disillusioned and more apprehensive. When he mentioned his concerns to his manager, the conversation focused mostly on what Kevin needed to do to get up-to-speed with the new technology. What Kevin wanted was help in getting himself mentally tuned-up for all of these changes. After a few days of careful reflection, Kevin handed in his resignation and worked for a year in his brother's art supply store until he found the kind of job he really wanted.

3. *Freeze.* By far, this has become the most popular of the three options and one of the major causes of productivity and quality problems in many companies. We convince ourselves that the best way to retaliate against what we perceive as an uncaring employer is to do as little work as possible. We do only what we have to do—no more, no less. Getting by without getting caught becomes our new performance standard. We maintain a low profile and engage in CYA (Cover Your Anatomy) behav-

iors designed to ensure that we do not get implicated if something goes wrong.

This is the option Debra K. decided to take while trying to figure out exactly what to do now that the bank she works for has merged with one of their largest competitors. Her work group has been downsized, and the volume of loan applications has increased dramatically. Debra is doing her best to stay ahead, but the quality of her work has been slipping. She is beginning to realize that she is caught in a vicious cycle: To make sure she keeps her job, she is taking on more than she can handle and making mistakes that could cause her to lose her job. Debra decided on a three-part plan: Start saying no to some of the less important tasks, go back as close as possible to the old standards and work expectations, and be prepared to defend whatever she is doing whenever anyone questions her performance. Debra cannot afford to lose her job. Surviving has become her number one priority.

Freezing might be easier than fight or flight; but in the long run it is the most dangerous and the most harmful choice of all because we run the risk of losing our initiative and destroying our job satisfaction.

The problem with all of these options is that they are reactive rather than proactive. Without some careful thinking, they are potentially career-ending choices. The risks usually outweigh the benefits. What is needed is a new approach, a career-building strategy called flourish.

Flourish

In this optimistic and enthusiastic approach, you and your manager work together to identify and capitalize on new opportunities. In environments where there is more work to do and fewer people to do it, many individuals are stepping up to the challenge and saying, "What can I do to help myself and my company succeed?" The process may not be an easy one, but more and more people are looking for ways to make productive contributions to their organizations so that they can feel good about the work they do. Many organizations and their managers try to foster this spirit of collaboration, teamwork, and mutual respect. By trying to flourish in their present jobs, many employees decide that the time has come for them to take responsibility for their own work lives.

Elena Rubiales, a technical consultant for a national wireless service provider, typifies this new spirit:

> Versatility and enthusiasm are important behaviors and attitudes
> for me. I don't just want a job—I want my career to be a positive

aspect of my life. Challenges are important to me. Believe it or not, I enjoy the endless emergencies, complaints, and impossible deadlines. My idea of the perfect workday is to walk in in the morning, start work, look at my watch, and realize it's time to go home. I want to be challenged to use every bit of brain power that I have to solve as many issues of the day as I can. And then I want to go home to an equally interesting social life.

I think my superiors will be looking for successful project results based on my ability to plan and negotiate despite difficult schedules and insufficient resources. I have the luxury of working in an industry whose competitiveness and technology fascinate me. I am really enjoying my work.

If you are currently dealing with difficult pressures at work and have decided that flight, fight, or freeze are not the best options for you, there are a number of specific actions you can begin to take to help you flourish and feel successful in your job. These actions are described in greater detail in the pages that follow. If things are currently going well for you at work, you can also benefit from understanding and practicing these new work habits—behaviors and skills you can develop and take with you throughout your working life. There are specific techniques you can use to demonstrate to others your interest and ability to be effective, efficient, and self-reliant. Regardless of where you are on your company's organizational chart, no matter if your role is manager or individual contributor, learning these new work habits will help you move into the next century with confidence and a sense of control.

This book has been designed to help you understand and apply techniques that may improve how you feel about going to work each day. There are eleven chapters—one for each of the new behaviors recommended—and a final chapter for a brief self-assessment. Chapters One and Two focus on doing the right things and balancing multiple demands on your time and resources. Chapters Three and Four emphasize teamwork—especially how you can sharpen your communication skills and develop productive relationships with the right people. Chapter Five outlines techniques for using a problem-centered approach to resolve conflicts, and Chapter Six describes problem-solving and decision-making techniques that can make a difference in the way you take charge of your own job. Chapters Seven and Eight highlight ways you can be innovative and flexible when you are dealing with change. Chapter Nine suggests ways you can take responsibility for your job performance. Chapter Ten encourages you to apply some of these "ownership" techniques to your own job and career. Chapter Eleven reviews some of the book's key concepts in a way that will allow you to do a brief self-assessment about how ready you are to move forward confidently into the next century.

Most of us can expect to spend close to 100,000 hours of our lives on the job. We hope the few hours you spend reading this book will make some of those working hours more productive and fulfilling.

1

Do What Your Company Is Paying You to Do

There is nothing so useless as doing efficiently that which should not be done at all.

—Peter F. Drucker, management guru

In her national bestseller, *The Overworked American* (HarperCollins, 1992), Juliet B. Schor documented that the amount of time people were spending at their jobs had risen steadily in the previous twenty years. Americans reported having only sixteen-and-a-half hours of leisure time each week after taking care of job and household obligations. Work hours were already longer than they were forty years ago, and today, many people will attest that their time at work has increased even more since the beginning of this decade. Today, most people work one month a year more than they did twenty years ago, and the average workweek is now about fifty-two hours.

In addition to longer work hours, there is greater pressure to use time wisely, a fact of life made even worse by downsizing, reengineering, and other company initiatives that have created more demands on fewer people. It has become much more stressful to accomplish what occasionally seem like unrealistic expectations.

According to Rob Hartwell, Senior Consultant for Custom Software Practices, self-discipline becomes an important part of the effort:

> It's very easy to get bogged down with technical details. I need to constantly step back and look at the big picture to make sure I'm on course. This means setting goals and reviewing them often. I start with short-term, tactical goals. Then I work

through each goal to make sure it is measurable and achievable. The process is not complicated. I just need to be sure I make the time to do it.

More than ever before, the challenge is to understand your work priorities, manage your time effectively, and determine the best way to produce high-quality results your company expects from you. There is less room for error and a greater need to do the right thing right the first time. Your work probably has greater visibility now, and you will be held accountable for contributing your share to your work group's collective efforts.

Regardless of where you are on your company's organization chart, it is more important than ever for you to understand your company's big picture and then develop a personal sense of how you fit in with these broader corporate objectives. This perspective will require a bottom-line focus similar to one that you probably use when you are contracting with someone for service. For example, when you are doing business with an automobile mechanic or a home improvement professional, you make decisions about the quality, the timing, and the cost of the services you are interested in buying. You need to use the same type of thinking at work so you can determine what is critical, urgent, and cost-effective about your job. You need to understand what your company is really paying you to do and how you can achieve these priority goals.

To help you succeed during these difficult, changing times, there are several action steps you can take to define your most important goals and prioritize your current work activities. Start by finding out more about your company's mission or purpose. Ask yourself, "Why is my company in business?" Try to obtain a useful answer by reading your company's mission statement, annual reports, and any other information that will help you get a better idea about your company's current priorities. Then try to understand how your own department or work group fits into this broad view. Ask, What are you and your immediate coworkers doing to contribute to your company's overall objectives? Then continue this downward funneling technique to focus on how you can contribute to the right organizational and departmental priorities.

Highlight some of your key ideas on the chart in Figure 1-1, then ask yourself some tough questions about the role you are playing in your company's current efforts.

- What specifically does your company expect from you?
- How will you know if you are making a satisfactory contribution to your company's success?

Figure 1-1. Understanding your company's mission, purpose, and goals.

The Big Picture

The Bottom Line

- How do you and your immediate manager currently measure your performance and your value to your company?
- What part do you play on your current work team?
- What results do you need to produce to feel effective and successful?
- What behaviors do you need to demonstrate to feel that you are doing your work efficiently?

Answering these questions will provide a bottom-line perspective and help you develop a personal vision, a sense of purpose about what is critical, urgent, and cost-effective about your job. More than ever before, it is critical for you to understand exactly what your company is paying you to do (the bottom line in Figure 1-1) so that you can achieve those priority goals and not waste your time on activities that may no longer contribute to or support what your organization is trying to accomplish.

One technique for clarifying your sense of purpose at work is to distinguish between acceptable and exceptional performance. Look at the chart in Figure 1-2. Start at the bottom of the chart by stating what you need to do to keep your job. This minimum requirement is the baseline that usually describes the most critical and urgent components of your job. You may also include some quality dimensions (How good does my work have to be to pass basic specifications?) and cost factors (How will I know if I am providing a fair day's work for the money I am being paid?).

Once you have determined the most critical bottom-line requirements of your job, you will be able to expand your thinking about other ways you can make a significant contribution to your company's success. Most people are not content with performing minimally; they are motivated by identifying aspects of their job that are more interesting, challenging, and valuable. Take a look at your description of acceptable performance, and then ask yourself how you can move toward exceptional performance by improving the quantity, quality, time, and cost factors associated with your job.

There are a number of critical outcomes you are being paid to deliver. Read your job description and discuss your current duties and responsibilities with your manager and anyone else who has influence over your job performance. Once you have defined required or desired results, determine specific actions, techniques, and behaviors that will help you deliver expected outcomes. Your list may include special projects, temporary assignments, new priorities, or routine activities you do every day to meet your company's expectations and earn your paycheck.

Remember, it is extremely important for you to make sure you are doing the right things right the first time. Check that the things you enjoy

Figure 1-2. A sense of purpose: defining what you need to do to succeed and excel.

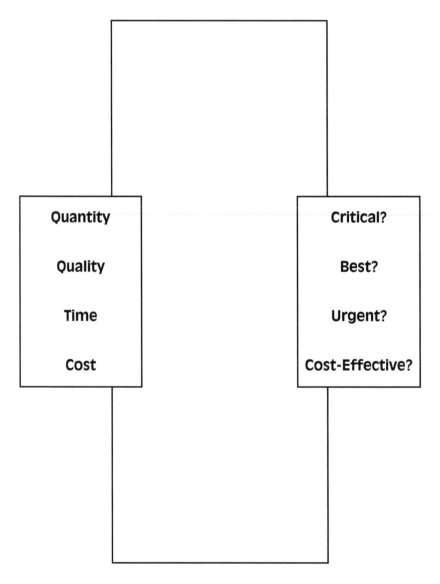

Exceptional Performance

Quantity	Critical?
Quality	Best?
Time	Urgent?
Cost	Cost-Effective?

Acceptable Performance

doing or are comfortable doing are still what your company needs from you. Doing something out of habit or because you have always done it in a particular way may not be the best way now. Make sure you are providing results to all the people who are depending on you. Include on this list your supervisor, coworkers, customers, and anyone else you interact with on a regular basis.

Once you have made your list of goals and priorities—ways that you believe you can contribute to your company's objectives—meet with your manager to set individual goals, clarify key performance areas, and reach agreement about what you are expected to accomplish during a defined time period. Your work goals are mutually agreed-upon performance outcomes that help you understand what you have to do to ensure that your actions and priorities are in alignment with company plans and initiatives.

For Dorothy Meyers of SmithKline Beecham, this approach helps her concentrate on important day-to-day activities:

> Goals are a very important aspect of my life. Therefore, I remain focused on them. I write them on paper and make them my to-do list. The to-do list is a clearly written blueprint of daily activities and is reviewed and revised daily. The to-do list includes achievable goals, "quick wins," in addition to goals that cause me to stretch.

Writing down your goals will help you understand and remember them. Your written goals then become a working document that you and your manager can use throughout the year for coaching, feedback, and progress reports. Your annual goals are not intended to be your complete job description. They are the most important areas necessary for you to focus on right now. You should review, discuss, and revise your goals regularly so that you stay current about what you should be working on at all times. If your manager is too busy to initiate a goal-setting conversation with you, this may be one of those occasions when you need to outline your thoughts and present them in a brief meeting (that you schedule) or in a short memo (asking for a fast response). By taking the initiative, you are demonstrating to your manager that you want to be sure you are working on the right projects and priorities.

❖ ❖ ❖ ❖ ❖

CASE STUDY

Barbara is overwhelmed by the number of new projects that have become her responsibility as a result of a recent downsizing

in her company. She feels she is now doing the work of at least three people, and she tells others that she feels as if she is treading water just to stay ahead. She is working longer hours and enjoying her work less. No sooner does she finish one task than two or three others require her attention.

Barbara has worked in time-crunch situations before, but this one is different. There does not seem to be any hope for a break, no light at the end of the tunnel. Barbara and her manager, Ralph, had set goals and priorities earlier in the year. Now, all of their planning has been replaced by a steady flow of new work that takes precedence over what they had determined were realistic goals and objectives. Barbara knows that Ralph is also feeling inundated by the incredible workflow his team is now required to deliver. Barbara has been working for this company for twelve years and has always enjoyed her work. But now, something has to give or she will have to start looking for a new job.

Your Analysis

Before reviewing Barbara's approach to this problem, write down some of your ideas about this situation. What would you do and why?

_____

_____

_____

The Employee's Actions

Because Barbara realized she was becoming paralyzed by her own indecision about which projects to attack first, she took a step back to get a broader view of all the work that needed to be done. Instead of pushing forward to finish several tasks at the end of one Friday afternoon, she blocked out two hours of her time to take a panoramic view of her work landscape. She stacked individual project outlines and assignments into seven different piles. On the top of each stack she placed a piece of colored paper containing critical information—date received, targeted date for completion, priority rating (A, B, or C), degree of complexity (high, moderate, low), and need for additional resources or support.

Once she completed the project cover sheets, Barbara shifted her focus to what she called "consequences of failure": What happens if my work does not meet the quantity, quality, time, and cost required? What will the impact be on me, my manager, my company, and our customers if I miss deadlines, run over budget, or cut corners with quality or accuracy?

Using this additional information, Barbara reprioritized two of the projects and changed one of her ratings from a "B" to a big question mark; this was definitely one she needed to talk to her manager about at their planned meeting Monday afternoon. Before leaving for the weekend, Barbara made a quick checklist of how she thought her work could be organized for the next few months. She listed all of her projects in priority order and briefly described her understanding of quality, time, and cost factors. She would talk to Ralph about whether there was any room for negotiation on these factors. She would make it clear that if there was no flexibility on the three highest priority projects, she would need some leeway on the three lowest priority assignments, such as more time to complete the projects or additional money to bring in temporary help or some modest changes in the level of quality required. Barbara's bottom line for the meeting with Ralph was: "I cannot get all of this work done effectively and efficiently without your guidance and support."

Finally, Barbara planned to discuss the project with the question-mark priority. One of the things she had discovered by taking this big-picture look at her work was that this one project, and all the tasks associated with it, might not be necessary anymore in the restructured organization. Barbara was pleased with this new insight. Eliminating this one project would save her at least five hours each week. She would also be able to remove the monthly report from her to-do list, a task that she disliked and always put off until the last minute. Barbara realized that she was on the verge of getting her priorities in order, that she had taken a major step toward organizing her goals and objectives, and that she was about to have a good weekend. She was prepared for her meeting with Ralph and knew he would appreciate the groundwork she had laid for their meeting.

❖ ❖ ❖ ❖ ❖

Remember that you share responsibility with your manager to ensure that the tasks you are working on are the ones most critical to your company's success. Excellent performance comes when you understand clearly what you have to do. Because the most frequent cause of poor performance is a lack of clarity about what is expected, not a lack of skills or a willingness to contribute, it is vitally important for you to understand what others expect from you.

Setting goals, therefore, is a continuous process in which you work with your manager to identify key business processes, determine priorities, decide on ways to measure your performance, and clarify individual goals for the year. The process should allow for flexibility and adaptability. Many people have found the mnemonic SMART helpful in developing and discussing good goals:

$$\textbf{S}\text{pecific}$$

$$\textbf{M}\text{easurable}$$

$$\textbf{A}\text{chievable}$$

$$\textbf{R}\text{elevant}$$

$$\textbf{T}\text{ime-Bound}$$

A performance requirement is *specific* if it states what is to be done and describes behaviors that can lead to the attainment of the goal. Starting your goal statement with an action verb (make, produce, write, build, complete, check, create, etc.) can help you use language that is specific and concrete. If it helps you, discuss and then list the activities you will need to do to achieve the goal.

A goal should be *measurable*. How well something is done is usually determined by its timeliness, accuracy, cost, and completeness. While some jobs lend themselves more easily to quantitative analysis, all goals should be written so that you can determine reasonably whether they have been reached. There are two types of measurements:

1. *Results* measures tell you and others what work is getting done. They are used to monitor the outputs of the work process so that these outputs meet company requirements. Results measures focus on accomplishments, such as total sales, on-time shipments, or number of new products.

2. *Process* measures indicate how work is getting done. They are used to ensure that you are doing what has to be done to achieve the desired outcomes.

A goal must be interesting, meaningful, and motivating to you. It must not be unreachable or beyond what can be reasonably expected of you. Performance requirements should be *achievable*, but they should also challenge and encourage you to give the most of your talent, ability, and energy. You should feel comfortable discussing with your manager whether you have the authority, resources, and capability to achieve a particular goal.

All performance goals should be *relevant*—because they support the mission, purpose, and strategy of the organization and your particular department or work unit. Ideally, you should review your goals with your manager after specific department goals have been passed down from higher levels in the company.

Once you and your manager have agreed on your goals, you should also clarify your priorities. If everything you are trying to accomplish has a "high priority" rating, you really do not have a priority system. If everything is critical and urgent, flipping a coin may be the only way to decide what you should do first. Such a haphazard approach to setting priorities can lead to frustration and misplaced energy.

A more systematic approach can help you determine your priorities and discuss them with others. One of the most common approaches is to focus on the importance and urgency of a goal so that you can give it an appropriate priority rating. Answering a few brief questions like the following can help you sort out priorities quickly and accurately:

- Is this goal critical to your company's success?
- Is this goal urgent enough to give it your immediate attention?

Finally, a goal should be *time-bound*—an activity, task, or process that must be completed by a particular date, on a regular schedule or on a routine basis. You should know when or how often specific tasks need to be completed. Adding a time dimension, like a deadline or target date, will help you confirm a goal's priority and provide a point of reference for you as you create a schedule and decide how to spend your available time.

Goals should be documented so that you can monitor your own performance and measure your progress. Such a self-monitoring system allows for ongoing evaluation, improvement, and development. You and your manager share responsibility for maintaining alignment, achieving success, and identifying areas where you need to shift or reexamine priorities.

So it is important to develop goal statements and then review them periodically to make sure you are using your time, energy, and resources effectively. Goals are not something you *do*. You do activities that lead to the accomplishment of goals, which makes planning an important part of this success formula. The following case study demonstrates how a conscientious employee used the goal-setting process to deal with a potentially difficult problem.

❖ ❖ ❖ ❖ ❖

CASE STUDY

Colin H. is a customer service representative for a computer software company that recently decided to discontinue its 800 number for technical support. Colin's manager knows that this decision will have a significant impact on current customers and may also affect the company's ability to attract new customers. He has asked Colin to develop a goal statement and an action plan that will help them deal with this change and minimize as many negatives as possible. The company's policy change is a major financial decision that needs to be made, and the company is depending on excellent employees like Colin to make it work.

Your Analysis

Before reviewing Colin's approach to this problem, take a few minutes to write down some of your ideas about a solution. What would you do and why?

_____

_____

_____

The Employee's Actions

Colin began the process by asking himself focused questions about the short-term impact of this decision:

- Which customers will be most affected by this change?
- Which customers will be most upset?
- What will my customers want or need from me?
- What will my best customers want or need from me?

- What options can I offer my customers?
- Can I provide certain valued customers anything special?
- What's the best way for me to inform my customers?
- What information do I need to have for these discussions?

These focused questions helped Colin identify many of the key issues he knew he would need to deal with in the next few months. They made it easier for him to develop a step-by-step action plan to communicate with his customers. He was then able to review the plan with his manager. Together they reviewed Colin's other current goals, changed the priorities of several of them, and made certain that this new situation got the highest priority attention for at least the next six months.

❖ ❖ ❖ ❖ ❖

There are many reasons people do not achieve even their most important goals. One of the most common reasons is that they do not plan carefully enough and fail to discuss their goals and priorities with the appropriate people—anyone who can affect your plans or anyone who will be affected by your actions. To test your own skills, write in your own words your understanding of one of your current goals. Use the space below to practice using the SMART guidelines:

Specific. What are you trying to produce or accomplish and how? ___

_____

Measurable. How will you know you have accomplished the objective or that you are moving in the right direction? _____

_____

Achievable. What resources and authority do you need? _____

_____

Relevant. How will this objective affect company or department activities? _____

_____

Time-Bound. When or how often does this objective need to be accomplished? _____

_____

Now use the goal-setting worksheet in Figure 1-3 to define your three or four most important goals. Once you have listed them, use the following questions to make sure you have prioritized them accurately:

- Which goals are most supportive of your company's mission, purpose, and strategic objectives?
- If you could accomplish only two of your goals, which ones would you choose?
- Which of your goals will yield the highest payoff—first, to your company, and then, to you?
- What would happen if you do not achieve these goals? What negative consequences would occur?

Your goals will help you move forward in a certain direction. But not every goal should be pursued at the same speed. Once you have established a goal, you need to place a value on it. The value should be based primarily on what must be done, not on what you prefer or enjoy doing. Once you have placed a value on the goal, you have established its priority. Make sure that what you think is important is consistent with what others in the organization need from you.

As you begin to develop a clearer understanding of your goals and priorities, remember to factor in other people's goals and priorities, especially if their deadlines are different from yours. You may have conflicting ideas about what has to be done, by whom, and by when. Often, your plate can be completely full, and it may seem that too many things are competing for your time. That is when prioritizing becomes essential and when communicating your short-term plans and activities becomes crucial to you, your manager, and your coworkers.

Finally, if you are trying to juggle many activities, you may want to list some of your current tasks and determine whether your assessment of priorities agrees with that of your manager and other key employees. The chart in Figure 1-4 provides a format for you to rank your top ten tasks, decide whether they are "must do" or "should do" responsibilities, and identify any discrepancies you will need to discuss with others who may be depending on you for results.

Remember, whatever you are trying to achieve, you cannot do it

Figure 1-3. Goal-setting worksheet.

Goal Description

    What? _____

    For Whom? _____

    When? _____

    Priority? _____

Goal Description

    What? _____

    For Whom? _____

    When? _____

    Priority? _____

Goal Description

    What? _____

    For Whom? _____

    When? _____

    Priority? _____

Goal Description

    What? _____

    For Whom? _____

    When? _____

    Priority? _____

Figure 1-4. Balancing multiple demands.

Your Top 10	Your Ranking	Any Discrepancies?
	Must Do vs. Should Do	

1.	___	___	___
2.	___	___	___
3.	___	___	___
4.	___	___	___
5.	___	___	___
6.	___	___	___
7.	___	___	___
8.	___	___	___
9.	___	___	___
10.	___	___	___

alone. Ultimately, you are responsible for what you accomplish and the actions you take every minute of every day. But your success takes teamwork, getting commitments from others, integrating your plans and actions with theirs, and discussing your goals and priorities with anyone who can affect your performance. A Leadership Development Consultant with a major computer software company describes setting goals and priorities as her major challenge:

> So many things need attention, and there is only me. I need to do a lot of exploration with my superiors and my client groups. I need to understand their highest priorities and figure out how I can leverage opportunities so that most clients' highest priorities can be addressed quickly. Then I need to get clear with peo-

ple about what I can provide to support their efforts in a way that will satisfy them and me. In some cases, it's an educational process because many people have never had to worry about getting agreement about shared priorities.

Over the years, many experts have researched and reported on why people do not achieve their goals. If you think about a situation in which you were unable to achieve a goal, you will probably identify one or more of the most common reasons. For example, some people do not take time to ask questions about their goals or confirm that they understand them completely. It is what many people would call "lack of a clearly defined purpose," which can produce what a colleague calls "false starts." He gets going one way and then finds out he was not really clear about what he was supposed to be doing. For example, last week his boss asked him for a cost estimate on a pending project. He spent hours on research before his boss stopped by and clarified his request: "Just give me a ballpark guess, not a full report. We can fine-tune your estimate later." My friend realized that he had wasted a lot of time by not asking for a specific description of the task his boss wanted him to do.

Conflicting priorities is another big reason why people do not accomplish their goals. Many people are not good at juggling things, and they often have to worry not only about what is important to them but what others have identified as urgent or critical goals. Coordinating your priorities with others can be very time-consuming and challenging. It is an essential step, however, if you want to be successful.

Procrastination is another reason people do not achieve their goals. Sometimes people can talk themselves out of doing even those things they once thought were vital to their success if they are afraid they are going to fail or fall short of their goal. They can convince themselves that they did not really fail—they just gave in to some other pressing priority. On the other hand, fear of success is another reason why goals are not achieved. People occasionally waste time and energy worrying about how different their lives might be if they actually reach a level of success they are working hard to achieve. In some cases, this fear of success either slows down their efforts or derails them altogether from reaching their planned destination.

Lack of personal organization can also be an obstacle to goal accomplishment. You probably know people at work who cannot get things done because they cannot find what they are supposed to be working on. Things are always buried under piles of clutter, and they are always trying to dig out and catch up. Sometimes, when you take the time to talk to these disorganized people, you will find that your conversations get back to defining goals, priorities, and the actions or activities that will help you and them accomplish your work group's goals. You may also be amazed at how often your coworkers have unrealistic expectations about their work goals. It may be surprising to learn how many people have become what we used to call "workaholics"—all work and no play, all work and no life—at their desks from dawn to dusk.

Which brings us to the last reason why goals are not achieved—failure to integrate professional and personal activities. Things can get out of balance, and it can become too easy to work hard at the wrong things. Many people have work goals and personal goals that are in conflict with each other. Work is an important and potentially satisfying part of our lives but it is not and should not be everything! Personal and work goals must be integrated.

Tina Hartwell, an internal consultant for a major high-tech firm, works hard to achieve the kind of balance she needs:

> I try to take a bigger-picture look at my whole-life priorities. We identify ourselves by what we do. I am in a phase of my life where I need to look at myself as a whole person. I do volunteer work because it is important for me to give something back to my community. I need to balance my work with my home life so that there is always room for my husband and other members of my family.
>
> At work, setting goals is pretty clear. I focus on what's important and don't spend too much time on things that add less value. I make a list of my current activities, and then I do a cost/benefit analysis to make sure what I am doing is worth doing. I check back to see how I am doing every week.
>
> I try this same technique at home. I ask myself whether what I am planning to do is really more important than something else: What will I miss by doing one thing instead of another?

You must find the right balance to stay focused on what is most important in your life so that you can coordinate what you do for a living with how you want to live. Goals and priorities are what will keep you going in the best direction. Therefore, it is critical for you to understand why you do the things you do:

- What motivates you?
- What do you hope to accomplish in your job?
- Do you know what you want to be doing a year from now?

- Do you have a plan for moving along the path you would most like to take?
- How does your current job fit into that plan?
- What part does your work play in your personal or family life?
- Does your job provide the satisfaction you want?
- Does it meet your current and future needs?

These are significant questions that influence your behaviors and will help you decide how you want to use your time and how committed you are to the job you are currently doing.

Clarify your personal and professional expectations, needs, and interests. Determine what you expect from your job. Understand what motivates you: money, power, affiliation, achievement, personal growth, a comfortable environment. Make sure your expectations are realistic, challenging, and achievable. Then put your work into a healthy perspective.

In the next chapter, we will examine how you can use the resources (including time) you need to make a meaningful contribution to your company's mission and objectives. For now, knowing what you can do to help make your organization successful and then doing it will automatically increase your value to the company. And when you increase your value to the company, you set yourself on a path for personal and professional success.

2

Balance Multiple Demands on Your Time and Resources

I must govern the clock, not be governed by it.
—Golda Meir, former Prime Minister of Israel

To feel a sense of accomplishment at work, you must understand what it will take for you to succeed. You must be able to describe (and then negotiate for) the tools and resources you need to accomplish your defined objectives. In work environments where budget and cost controls have become important concerns, you need to know how to balance multiple demands, manage your time better than ever, and use limited resources as efficiently as possible.

You and your manager will evaluate the quality of your job performance by using two overall measurement criteria—effectiveness and efficiency. Each of these factors has a specific focus that you will want to incorporate into your daily work activities:

- Effectiveness is selecting the right goals from a set of possibilities and then achieving them.
- Effectiveness means getting results.
- Efficiency assumes you have picked your goals and requires you to determine the best way to achieve the goals you have decided to pursue.

Effectiveness is doing the right job; efficiency is doing the job right. Once you have decided what you need to do and how you intend to do it, take a few minutes to review the goals and priorities you worked on in the previous chapter. If everything is in sync, this is a good time to look at the specific tasks you are currently doing to meet your stated goals. It is also a good opportunity to check the way you are managing your time. The time-analysis worksheet in Figure 2-1 can help you take a quick look at how you have decided to distribute your work.

Step 1. List your current work activities on the chart and estimate how much time you spend on each activity each day. Use hours/minutes, and be as precise as possible.

Step 2. Circle those activities that are the most important ones in helping you meet your highest priority goals.

Step 3. Review the amount of time you spend on the circled activities, and decide whether you are devoting enough time to these more important tasks.

Step 4. Review the amount of time you spend on the noncircled activities, and decide whether you are devoting too much time to nonessential tasks.

Figure 2-1. A time-analysis worksheet.

Work Activity	Time Spent on Each Activity					Weekly Totals
	M	*T*	*W*	*T*	*F*	
Most time-intensive activity each day						

Step 5. Decide whether your most time-intensive daily activities are the right ones.

Once you have a picture of one week's activity, you can make informed decisions about the benefits and limitations of your current work configuration. You may want to shift certain tasks to different time slots. You may decide to spend more or less time on activities that are getting inappropriate attention now.

As you examine your time management practices, be sure that you do not confuse activity with results. Busy-ness is not always the best measure of what's good for business. You need to focus, instead, on outcomes and bottom-line contributions. On a regular basis, you need to ask yourself the following questions:

- Did my work today add value to what my company is trying to accomplish?
- Did I devote enough time to my most important goals and priorities?
- Did I do things out of habit without thinking about their significance or potential impact?
- Did I take shortcuts that may have affected my efficiency (doing things right) or damaged my effectiveness (getting the right results)?
- Am I managing my time well or do I need to make adjustments to the way I have divided my work?

Remember the exercise you did in the last chapter about acceptable vs. exceptional performance. How much time will it take for you to be successful, and are you willing to make that commitment?

If you are chronically pressed for time, there are several time management techniques you may want to try:

- Schedule planning time for yourself. Don't tell yourself you are too busy to plan. One of the reasons you may be too busy is that you have not taken enough time to plan your day, your week, your life.

- Develop a schedule for yourself by using a calendar, one of those convenient datebook planners, or an electronic organizer. Start by blocking out time you have no control over—time that has already been committed for activities like meetings or training classes. List important deadlines on your schedule, and remember to allow yourself some time for relaxation and nonwork activities.

- Avoid overcommitting yourself. Learn to say "no" or "not now."

- Know when you are usually at your peak energy level, and schedule your work accordingly. This is an individual choice. However, if you know you are not a morning person, you may want to put off key meetings and important decisions until you are ready to participate or function at your maximum ability.

- Analyze your current activities so you can deal with common time wasters—those habitual tasks or nonproductive practices that can undermine your overall effectiveness.

A time waster is anything that keeps you from doing something that is more important to you. By its very name, a time waster is an inappropriate use of one of your most valuable assets. Time wasters are different for each of us. A ten-minute walk around the company parking lot may be a time waster for one person, but a chance to reflect about an upcoming meeting or a way to relieve stress for someone else.

There are ten common time wasters people usually describe when they are asked to analyze how and why they lose precious minutes and hours from their daily lives. Circle the ones on the clock face in Figure 2-2 that may be problems for you right now. Then review some suggestions for dealing with these time wasters.

Figure 2-2. Common time wasters.

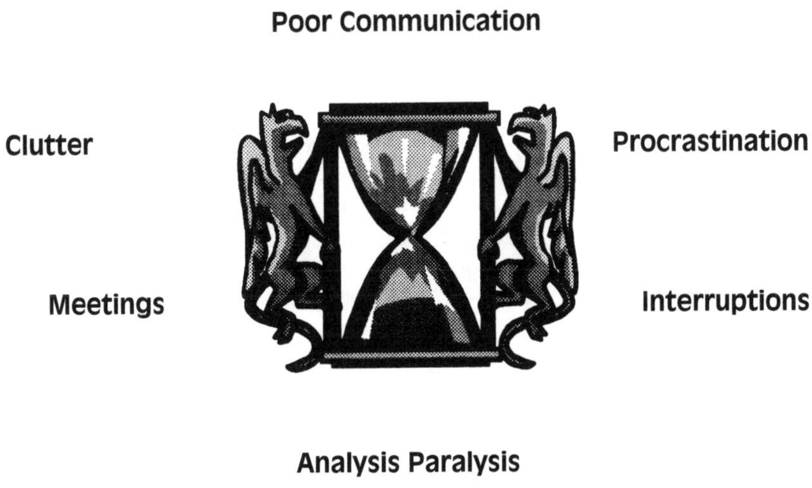

Poor Communication

Clutter   **Procrastination**

Meetings   **Interruptions**

Analysis Paralysis

Time-Waster #1: Poor Communication

Some experts have said that poor communication practices—giving incomplete or inaccurate information to someone—is the number one reason for lost time in American companies today. By not getting the message right the first time, individuals have to do work over, correct mistakes that could have been avoided, or make major midstream revisions to their project schedules and priorities.

By not paying careful attention to their communication efforts, people run the risk of wasting time on unnecessary activities. For example, Maureen S., a purchasing representative for a large medical facility, recently described the following situation:

> My supervisor, Lee, asked me to do some research about additional computer equipment we have been thinking about getting for the department. He said he needed the information in two weeks for a meeting with senior management. We talked about the different types of equipment I would investigate, and I left the meeting feeling excited about this project. It would give me a chance to show off some of my best skills and might even give me a chance to get some visibility and recognition from upper management.
>
> So I jumped into this new assignment with enthusiasm, even shifting a few other priorities so that I could make time for this investigative work. In the next ten work days, I spent at least thirty-five hours, close to half my available time, reading about different computers and talking to local suppliers. When I was finally satisfied that I had enough information, I wrote a comprehensive report comparing the top five computers for our specific needs and the top two suppliers based on their pricing policies and their customer support reputation. I was putting the finishing touches on my spiral-bound, forty-page report, when Lee stopped by and asked, "Do you have those figures I need for tomorrow's meeting?" I proudly handed him my report, the fruits of my hard work, and he said, "Wow, Maureen, this is much more than I expected. I really just need a few rough estimates about how much we need to budget for our department's computer equipment for the next three years. Do me a favor and give me a one-page breakdown of those numbers before you leave today."
>
> And that was it—no "thank you" for a great job, no recognition for my hard work. In fact, just the opposite. My reward for

the work I had done was more work, a summary of my report due by the end of the day. Lee and I had miscommunicated in a big way, and, once I had settled down, I tried to figure out why. Here are my conclusions:

- Lee knew what he wanted, but he had not made that clear to me. Our meeting was brief and hurried, and I think, in hindsight, that this one agenda item got lost in the shuffle. If Lee had simply said, "I need cost estimates for a budget meeting," I might have spent less time on my research.
- I heard what I wanted to hear. I created my own ideal sce-nario—an exciting project with new opportunities and chal-lenges. I should have asked some clarifying questions during the meeting, but I guess I wanted to believe that what I was hearing was what I wanted to do on this new assignment. In the long term, the research I did will be important to our department. Short-term, I wasted valuable time over the past two weeks, shifting attention away from tasks I now need to play catch-up with, and setting myself up for some personal disappointment about the praise I expected and the recognition I deserved. I learned an important lesson about the necessity of clear communication.

We will give additional attention to communication skills in the next chapter. For now, here are a few techniques that can help you overcome the time problems caused by poor communication:

- At the end of every conversation you have with anyone about a new work project or assignment, take the time to clarify the other person's expectations about your role and responsibilities. Ask open questions: "What do you need from me?" and "How do you want this information?" to be sure you understand the exact nature, scope, and importance of this particular task.
- Repeat or paraphrase what the other person has said so that both of you agree on the message you are taking away from the conversation. Sometimes a brief note summarizing the outcome of the meeting can help guarantee that there are no misunderstandings. It takes a few extra min-utes to wrap up these types of discussions effectively, but the time spent at this point in the process can save you valuable time and energy.
- If you are not certain about how a new task or project fits into your busy schedule, take the time to sort out and readjust priorities. The worst

thing you can do is to leave this type of meeting with a mistaken impression about the importance of the project. Either you will underestimate its significance and disappoint someone else, or you will overestimate its significance and potentially disappoint yourself.

■ Take time to review what you have written before sending a memo or e-mail message. Because you do not have a face-to-face opportunity to clarify what you want the other person to get from your note, take care before you transmit it. If the content is important, consider a follow-up telephone call to confirm that the other person received and understands your message. If the content is very important and the receiver is accessible, consider a meeting rather than e-mail. For many people, e-mail has become a convenient alternative to meetings. Be sure, however, that your communication methods match the importance of your message.

Time-Waster #2: Procrastination

Most people procrastinate to avoid an unpleasant task, to postpone doing a job they think may be too difficult, to make sure they have management support before they begin, or to ensure the work they are about to do is really worth their effort. Sometimes certain tasks are not as interesting, challenging, or motivating as other assignments. Sometimes they seem too complex and overwhelming.

If you are an occasional or habitual procrastinator, try to determine why you are putting off a particular job. Once you have analyzed the cause of your hesitation, here are several time management techniques that can help you overcome it:

■ If the task at hand is an unpleasant one, admit it, and remind yourself how relieved you will be to have it finished. Then plunge in and get it done. When you have completed the job, reward yourself with a coffee break or a small victory cheer or just the satisfaction of crossing the task off your to-do list.

■ If the job is too difficult or complex, break it down into smaller tasks. Remember the old saying about the best way to eat an elephant is one bite at a time. By dividing larger projects into smaller parts, you can also build success one step at a time. Stay focused on each phase, and try not to worry about the whole project or how it will end. You can create and maintain momentum by taking a steady step-by-step approach.

■ If you are waiting for support from your manager, don't wait too long. Go ask for it or determine if you already have it. A friend recently described a situation in which she waited for two weeks to get a green light from her boss on a project that she was challenged to try. She was so excited about the prospect of this new activity that she did not realize she had been given the authority to begin earlier in the month. By the time she asked her manager about the status of the project, she was surprised to learn that she was already behind schedule.

■ If you are not certain the task ahead of you is really worth the effort, review your current priorities and check with your manager about the cost-benefit ratio of this particular job. You may decide that you are correct and that spending your time on other tasks is more beneficial. On the other hand, you may decide that you are avoiding the task because it is unpleasant, not as important as other things you like to do, or because it is something that you have inherited from another person and do not consider part of your job. If the task is a necessary one that is now part of your job, the best thing to do is add it to your schedule and get it done. Like the Nike commercial recommends—just do it! Stop wasting hours of time avoiding the task or debating its importance.

Organize your time to match your own energy level. Give yourself at least one hour during your peak time to work on your most important priority of the day. Another technique is to use some of your peak energy time to finish some of your unpleasant tasks. Your enthusiasm can carry you along and get you quickly through whatever tasks you like least. Even if your energy wanes later, you can usually maintain momentum better when you are working on a task you enjoy.

If you tend to procrastinate, don't put off addressing the causes and developing specific actions you can take to get things back on track.

Time-Waster #3: Interruptions

Interruptions come in different shapes and sizes. You may need to deal with unexpected visitors or telephone calls. Some disruptions may be urgent but not as important as the work you are trying to complete. For example, you learn that the order you placed for a computer package has been delayed, and you need to call another vendor. That task, however, may take secondary priority to the budget report your manager needs from you by noon today. The challenge is to handle the interruption as quickly as possible so you can return to your priority task. Some disruptions may be critical enough for you to shift your focus and devote a great deal of time to the new priority. This requires quick thinking and enough flexibility on your part to shift gears effectively. Even if handling the interruption takes more time than you can afford, it is important to step back and reassess what time you have left to resume the work you had been doing.

Keep track of the people and the events that interrupt you and cause you to readjust your schedule. If there are interruptions that are unnecessary or unimportant, do whatever it takes to get control of them. Talk to the people who drop in and ask them to be more sensitive to your work schedule. You may not be able to manage random events that interfere with your plans, but if you keep track of them, you may notice trends or patterns that you can work into your plans. This type of contingency planning—"What could go wrong with my current schedule?"—can help make certain interruptions less stressful.

The best way to deal with unexpected visitors and telephone calls is to be clear about your own personal preferences. Start by making a quick assessment of the situation. Is it urgent, critical, or complex? Can you handle it quickly, or will it take more time than you can spare? If you need to deal with the interruption, note where you are in your own work so that you can return there easily. If you cannot deal with the interruption at this time, explain why to the person who has approached or called you. Be as precise and specific as you can:

- "I think I can help you, but right now I'm in the middle of something. Can I call you this afternoon and set up a time to get together?"
- "I'll need to look up some information to help you with your request. Can we block out an hour later this week so that I'll be better prepared to talk about these issues?"
- "I can't pull away from this report right now. Friday or Monday would be better days for me to focus on what I think may be a complex problem. Why don't you let me know what's good on your schedule, either of those days, and what you want me to bring to our meeting. Leave me a note today, and I'll confirm with you tomorrow."

If appropriate, suggest someone else who might be able to help if you can't. Keep track of any follow-up commitments you have made, and make sure you keep all of your promises. This will enhance your reputation as a dependable person who wants to be as helpful as possible even though your busy schedule may require some adjustments.

Time-Waster #4: Analysis Paralysis

There are several common reasons for this broad time-waster category, but the outcome is usually the same as an inability to decide exactly what to do next. In some cases, you may be so bombarded with data that it will take time for you to sort out all the details. This type of information overload has become more prevalent in our high technology world where facts, figures, and new data are so readily available. Access to this information can be especially detrimental if you tend to be a perfectionist. You can become paralyzed by waiting for one more piece of information, one more detail that will help you begin or continue your work. At some point, you will need to make a critical decision about whether the benefits of the final product you are perfecting is worth the time and energy you are investing in completing it.

Another certain sign that you may be suffering from some degree of analysis paralysis is the number of false starts you make on a task or project. If you find yourself rethinking your actions and going back to the drawing board to start again, you should examine what's causing your stop and start behaviors. One possibility is that you are letting different skills interfere with each other. For example, Katherine H. recently described how long it takes her to write a report about her monthly customer visits. She described the process this way:

> I start writing a description of what actually happened, but within a few minutes, I find myself editing and rewriting what I just wrote. This goes on for several minutes, and I make several attempts to state my ideas clearly. Then I give up. If I am writing notes long-hand, I usually crumple the page and start again. If I am doing the work on my computer, I usually delete what I have done, walk away for a few minutes, and start again later.
>
> When I mentioned this problem to a friend, he suggested that I was really trying to do two things at once and that I was mixing two different sets of skills—writing, which is a more creative activity, and editing, which is more analytical and logical. He suggested that I just push ahead with my writing and stay focused entirely on getting all of my ideas on paper or on the screen. He recommended that I go back when that's done to make changes, check for grammar and spelling, and refine what I have written. This new approach has saved me countless hours of time each month, and I no longer resist what has always been an unpleasant task for me.

Analysis paralysis can also occur when you simply have too much to do, and you are uncertain about how to sort out what to do next. Perhaps you have made too many commitments or promises. Perhaps you have spread yourself too thin by saying "yes" to too many things. It is easy to do, especially if you are a conscientious person who wants to help others as much as you can. Or maybe you want to assure your manager that you can do a competent job even though there is more and more work to be done.

The challenge is sorting out your "must do" and your "might do" tasks. Part of the way to manage these time conflicts is to learn how to say "no" or "maybe" or "not now"—whatever words communicate your interest in helping when the task becomes a higher priority for you. Ask yourself and your manager if activities that have become part of your routine need to stay that way. For example, ask if a specific written report is still as necessary as it used to be. Can a monthly report become a quarterly one or a quarterly report an annual one? Look carefully at those habitual tasks you are currently doing and determine if there are less time-consuming options. Identify and eliminate nonessential tasks. Take a hard look in particular at those work items you enjoy doing the most. They have a way of taking up more time on your schedule than you may be able to afford to give them right now. Be careful not to volunteer for too many special project teams until you know exactly what you are committing yourself to do.

Which brings us back to some of the ideas from the previous chapter. The best way to manage your time and avoid analysis paralysis is to set goals, define priorities, and periodically evaluate whether your original plan is still working. Remember that goals are what determine how you spend your time. Setting goals will define what is most important for you to accomplish on a daily or weekly basis. Schedule adequate time for planning so that you spend minimal time on tasks that do not have a high value to you and your organization. Whenever necessary and possible, develop a contingency plan for dealing with potential problems. Anticipate what can go wrong and figure out the best way to prevent the problem from happening (fire prevention tactics) or to minimize its impact if it cannot be avoided (damage control). If you are currently working on different projects and different project teams, be sure to define your roles and responsibilities and determine which goals are most important to achieve.

Transfer your goals and priorities to a realistic work schedule. Wherever possible, combine similar activities. Consolidate activities that can be done in one manageable block of time. For example, you may want to make all of your telephone calls during one scheduled block of time each day. If you need to leave a message, you may also want to encourage people to return your call during a specific range of time so you can anticipate these interruptions. Have tasks available to work on if you have an unexpected break or some unanticipated free time. Some time management experts recommend rotating the type of work you are doing so that you have a nice variety of creative and routine activities. Establish periodic milestones to help you measure your progress and celebrate your successes. Remember that a schedule is a written promise to yourself to accomplish key tasks in a specific order. A formal schedule provides a good way for you to visualize your day or week and make any necessary adjustments. If your schedule looks too busy, make sure your priorities are getting ample attention.

If you are having problems with conflicting priorities, you may need help from others. Your manager may be the best person to ask, but prepare yourself for the conversation by reviewing the priority checklist from the previous chapter. By doing that, you will be able to offer your opinion about the best way to spend your time and energy. If the conflicting priorities are the result of new or changing requirements from coworkers or customers, try to work out an acceptable alternative with them. If you are not able to determine the best priority, you may need to ask your manager to break the tie for you. Remember to evaluate how you are using your time in terms of payoff and return on your investment.

Once you have broken any logjams in your daily schedule and gotten over your analysis paralysis, spend some time periodically monitoring your results. Ask yourself if you have achieved your most important goals and then determine the impact of not doing certain tasks. Adjust your priorities when necessary and fine-tune your schedule to accommodate any new developments. However, do not waste an inordinate amount of time making these decisions. Decide which tasks need to get done and allocate the time to do them.

Time-Waster #5: Meetings

When asked to describe their biggest time-wasters at work, many people put meetings at the top of the list. The reason is obvious: Many business meetings are poorly planned and conducted. Often, the participants are not sure what the meeting is about or why they have been asked to attend. The meeting leaders are not prepared and are easily distracted by attendees who have their own agendas. In terms of lost or wasted time, the results can be staggering. Very few of the ideas recorded at meetings are remembered at all; many of the ideas that are remembered are remembered incorrectly; most of the ideas requiring follow-up action never get implemented.

Meetings fail for a number of reasons:

- Lack of planning and preparation by both the leader and the participants.

- Conflicting or unclear objectives.
- Bad timing (people are distracted by other work priorities.
- No real need for a meeting in the first place.
- Too much meeting time and energy spent on nonproductive activities like venting, complaining, or finger-pointing rather than actual problem-solving.
- Participants arrive with negative feelings about meetings in general caused by too many other (unsuccessful) meetings. There is resistance and cynicism from the start.
- Reluctance to participate because the wrong people are invited.
- Too many people are invited there is not enough time for everyone to participate effectively.
- Participants are unclear about their role in the meeting or how they can contribute.

If you have any doubt about the quality of most meetings, think about a meeting you attended or conducted recently. Evaluate its effectiveness based on the following questions:

- Did you know the purpose of the meeting before you arrived? Was the purpose or objective stated at the beginning of the meeting?

  _____

- Did the meeting accomplish its objective and result in some relevant action? _____

- What could the meeting leader have done to make the meeting more effective and productive? _____

- What could the participants have done to make the meeting more effective? _____

If one of your current job responsibilities is to schedule and conduct meetings, make sure that any meeting you plan is necessary. Ask yourself whether a meeting is the best way to accomplish your objective and help you and your group move forward to achieve your goals. If the answer is "yes," then ask the following questions to make sure you get the maximum benefit for everyone involved:

- What is the purpose of this meeting?
- What positive changes would you like to see as a result of this meeting?

- Who should attend this meeting and why?
- What procedures or ground rules should you follow?
- When and where should the meeting be held to ensure minimum interruptions and promote maximum participation?
- What information should participants have prior to the meeting?
- How will the meeting activities and outcomes be recorded?

The meeting planner in Figure 2-3 can help you keep track of all the important components of any meeting you conduct.

If your primary or exclusive involvement with meetings is as a participant, remember that you share responsibility to make these events successful. There are several specific things you can do to get the most benefit from the meetings you are being asked to attend:

Before the Meeting

- If you are not certain about the nature and purpose of the meeting, ask someone who knows. The meeting leader is probably the best place to start.
- If you are unclear about why you have been invited, clarify the leader's expectations before you show up for the meeting.
- If there is an agenda, read it carefully and make any preparatory notes about topics or areas to which you can contribute.
- If there is reading or other preparatory work requested in advance by the leader, do it so that meeting time is not wasted on activities that should have been done earlier.

During the Meeting

- Participate to the best of your ability. Contribute your ideas, and do whatever you can to make the meeting successful.
- Monitor your own behavior to be sure you are not monopolizing conversations or overwhelming more passive participants.
- If you tend to be quiet or shy, look for safe opportunities to speak and respond enthusiastically when the leader or some other participant invites you to contribute.
- Take notes to ensure that you remember commitments or action items.
- Make sure your meeting behaviors are appropriate and helpful. Limit or eliminate unnecessary sidebar conversations with other participants. Avoid lobbying for a favorite position; once you have made your point, let it rest. Resist becoming argumentative, hostile, or stubborn in the face of resistance from others. Give the

Figure 2-3. Meeting planner.

Purpose: _____

Objective: _____

Who Should Attend: _____

Roles/Procedures: _____

Logistics: _____

When? _____

Where? _____

Agenda: Created _____ Distributed _____

Record Meeting Events: Self _____ Other _____

Possible Problems:

☐ With the time you have selected: _____

☐ With the place you have selected: _____

☐ With the meeting topics or agenda: _____

☐ With the people who will be attending and the roles you

  have asked them to play: _____

  _____

meeting leader enough leeway to manage healthy disagreements
and bring them to a positive conclusion.

- Stay focused on the stated meeting objectives, and do your best to
  help achieve them within the allocated time.

After the Meeting

- Review your meeting notes and transfer any action items or commitments to your calendar or schedule. If you have any questions

about target dates or new assignments, ask the meeting leader for clarification as soon as possible.

- Follow through on any promises you have made. Keep the meeting leader (or anyone else you have made a commitment to) informed about your progress or any problems you encounter.
- If invited to do so, give the meeting leader feedback about the meeting and make appropriate suggestions for improving future meetings.
- If asked, recommend agenda items for the next meeting, especially if there are issues you would like this group of people to address.

Remember that meetings have the potential to be one of your company's greatest time wasters. If eight employees gather for a nonproductive two-hour meeting, the organization has lost sixteen hours or two days of productivity. Consider other possible negatives: People leave the meetings discouraged and frustrated and waste even more time discussing how bad it was; people become cynical and resist volunteering for future project teams; people develop resentment and bear hidden grudges toward other participants who might have derailed the meeting. Whether you are the meeting leader or an invited participant, you have an important responsibility to make your meeting time-effective and efficient.

Time-Waster #6: Clutter

The ability to put your hands on exactly what you need when you need it has probably become more challenging then ever. If you are like most people, you are bombarded constantly by data, and information flows into your work area at an amazing pace from a variety of sources. E-mail has accelerated communication, but "snail mail" correspondence continues to arrive daily. Some people still prefer the office memo or some other type of written note, and these pieces of paper may get a place of honor at the top of your paperwork pile, at least until the next batch of mail arrives. Add to this clutter various company reports and magazine articles you intend to read when you have the time. Then find room for company announcements about new benefit packages or training programs. Finally, balance your growing pile with those miscellaneous items everyone tends to collect such as takeout menus from local restaurants, instructional manuals for computer equipment that is already obsolete, and office supply catalogs. If clutter is one of your major time wasters, make a decision now to get organized. As Christopher Robin says in A.A. Milne's *Winnie the*

Pooh, "Organization is what you do before you do something, so that when you do it, it's not all mixed up."

Set aside time to clean up your work space. Focus on what is most important to help you meet your current priorities. Sort and file papers that have accumulated during the past few days or weeks, and make decisions about them as you go along. Four separate piles should help you make your initial sorts. Make quick decisions and try to handle paper only once. Label each pile so that you know exactly where you want to put each item:

1. *Action Needed.* This pile contains items that require some decision, response, or future attention from you. This may be a good time to stack them in priority order. If quick action is required, make a note about how you want to respond—in person, on the telephone, or by e-mail.

2. *Completed.* This pile consists of items that, for one reason or another, no longer require your attention. Junk mail that you have been saving for a forgotten reason should be trashed immediately. Other items can be filed in folders labeled "Save for Marketing Conference" or "Good Ideas for Future Reports." The more descriptive and specific your labels, the easier it will be for you to recall and retrieve the contents later.

3. *For Others.* This pile contains items that you have been saving because they might be useful to someone else. Put the individual's name on each item so you can move it from your desk to the other person's desk as soon as possible.

4. *Undecided Now.* This is a catch-all pile for anything you cannot put in one of the first three piles. For now, keep this pile as small as possible, and do not let it distract you from getting most of your other papers arranged the way you want them.

Next, eliminate all the little notes and reminders you have accumulated around your work space. Transfer any important messages from scraps of paper or Post-it Notes to a safer place such as a to-do list that you will be more likely to refer to and less likely to lose.

A few months ago, I had coffee with a young salesperson in his fairly cluttered office. He had small mounds of bright Post-it Notes piled up all over his desk. Every time he put his coffee cup down, several scraps of paper would flutter away or flip over and attach themselves to the bottom of his cup. All I could think of was that I was witnessing some type of "survival of the fittest" response system in which the earliest message received—those buried safely at the bottom of the pile—would be the only ones he would be able to read clearly and call back.

A different type of system would have been better for him and might also work for you. Whether you do your to-do list on a computer, on a legal pad, in a calendar, or in one of those popular schedulers, such as an electronic organizer or Day Runner, you need a system that will allow you to access information quickly and effectively. The bottom line is that you need to organize those scraps of paper so that important information does not get lost in the shuffle or tossed into the trash with your morning coffee napkin.

The next step in dealing with clutter is to clear your work area of any nonessential tools. Find a better place to store the calculator you may use once a month, the stapler you use a few times a week, or the training manual you refer to only when you need to refresh your memory about some unusual policy or procedure. Sit at your work station, stretch out your arms, and move them in an arc until they meet. Include in this imaginary "half-circle" only those tools or resources that you depend on to do your job effectively every day. Make sure that what you need is readily at hand so that you do not waste time leaving your work area to get the critical tools of your trade. Keep your desk clutter-free by removing decorative items that can distract you from the tasks at hand. Keep family photos and other personal memorabilia to a minimum. Limit distractions so that you can stay focused on what you need to accomplish.

Keep only one project—your top priority for the moment—on your desk or at your work station. Keep other items off your desk until you are ready for them. The problem with stacking additional items on your desk is that you soon will not be able to forget or ignore them. Your mind will wander to these additional items that will eventually need your attention. Do not allow yourself to be distracted by other tasks because they are more interesting, enjoyable, or easier. Work on your top-priority task until it is completed to your satisfaction.

It is important for you to contribute to your company's success by meeting key objectives effectively, on time, and within budget. Keep those three measurement criteria—quality, time, cost—in mind with everything you do. They are the most common standards organizations use to evaluate their success.

❖   ❖   ❖   ❖   ❖

CASE STUDY

In the previous chapter, Colin H. developed a goal, strategy, and plan for dealing with a major change in the way his company provides technical support to its customers. After identifying key customers and the issues he would have to discuss with them, Colin met with his manager, reprioritized several other projects he had been working on, and began developing a schedule of action items and target dates. It is September 1, and the policy will be implemented November 30.

Your Analysis

Before reviewing Colin's approach to this problem, take a few minutes to write down some of your ideas about this situation. What would you do and why?

_____

_____

_____

_____

The Employee's Actions

Colin developed a six-step approach:

Step 1. List all my best customers and double-check the list with my manager and several coworkers to make certain I have not overlooked anyone. Target Date: September 8

Step 2. Decide what issues these preferred customers might have with our new approach and focus on any unique problems. Target Date: September 15

Step 3. Meet with tech support representatives and determine what options I have to offer my customers. Try to identify benefits that could make our service even better. Target Date: September 30

Step 4. Make telephone calls to customers explaining changes, listen to their concerns, and let them know I understand their needs. When necessary, schedule a return call to address their issues. Target Date: October 5 to October 30

Step 5. Mail company announcement to all customers. Include short personal note to select group who may want or need additional support. Target Date: November 5

Step 6. Be available for telephone calls from customers. Make certain that key customers have access to someone who can help when I am away from my desk. Target Date: November 15 to December 15

As Colin reviewed all the aspects of this new priority assignment, several things were obvious:

- Planning was a crucial part of the process and helped him define what outcomes he needed to accomplish.
- The defined outcomes helped Colin identify certain behaviors and skills he should use to achieve desired results. Some of these behaviors would require special attention because they were not activities that Colin used often on other projects. He would need to brush up on his telephone skills. He would need to manage his time more effectively. He would need to get help with his meeting management skills.
- It was soon clear to Colin that the way he approached this challenge—the *How* of his performance—would have a big impact on the results—the *What* of his efforts.

❖ ❖ ❖ ❖ ❖

If you feel you do not have adequate resources to achieve your goals, discuss what you need as soon as possible with those who have the ability and responsibility to support your efforts. Start by determining what additional resources you need (see Figure 2-4 for a helpful checklist). Once you have decided what you need more of and why, translate that information into language that will have a positive impact on your manager. For example:

- To complete this project on time, I will need more authority to call customers directly and not depend on someone from sales to contact them first.
- My current computer software is outdated. I can improve my response time by twenty percent with a fairly inexpensive upgrade.
- If you bring in a temporary file clerk, I can reduce our department's current backlog in less than two weeks. The cost of this additional resource might be less than our present overtime expenses.
- I am concerned about the quality of my telephone interactions with my customers. I often feel rushed and pressured by other less important priorities. With your help, I would like to block out two hours each morning to be used exclusively for telephone calls. That

would mean we would both have to concentrate on managing our time on other projects more efficiently.

Notice how these examples use the quality, time, and cost standards described above. These three measurement criteria should be important concerns when evaluating your own performance. Use them when organizing your work efforts, negotiating for additional resources, and planning to meet your key objectives. They will help you:

- Control time, expenses, and budget effectively.
- Plan and organize your work to produce maximum quantity and quality output.
- Coordinate your efforts effectively within and across work units.
- Routinely evaluate the costs and benefits of your projects and suggestions.
- Routinely plan for contingencies, reduce surprises, and anticipate potential problems.

Figure 2-4. Determining what resources you need to succeed.

Resource	Enough	More	Specific Conclusions
Equipment			
Tools			
People			
Materials			
Authority			
Other:			

- What do you need more of and why?

- How would you negotiate with your manager for the additional resources you need?

There is one key question you need to answer if you begin to feel overwhelmed by the volume or pace of your work: "Why am I doing this?" There are many constructive answers: "I am making a difference for my customers," "I am excited about helping my project team develop a new product or process," or "I am getting personal satisfaction from doing a task I did not think I was capable of mastering." There are also discouraging answers that you will need to address and resolve: "I don't know why I am doing this," "I have no choice, no other options," or "I'll lose my job if I don't."

It is critically important for you to clarify where and how work fits into your overall life priorities. Determine your key values and adjust your time commitments to match your needs. You may need to slow down in some areas or even stop giving valuable time to less important activities. If you tend to be impatient or impulsive, try to pace yourself. Step back occasionally to understand exactly what's going on with the way you are managing your time. Ask yourself some difficult questions:

- Do you have the right balance in your life and your work?
- Are urgent, but less important, matters taking up an inordinate amount of your time?
- Are you rushing through important tasks because you have spent too much time on less critical activities?
- Who is responsible for your current time crunches—you, your manager, or your family?
- Are you too available to people who may not be as sensitive to your priorities and needs as they should be?
- Are you able to walk away from work at the end of the day or does time-saving technology make you accessible around the clock?

In *The Overworked American,* Juliet Schlor points out that no evidence exists to show that longer hours lead to higher productivity. In fact, the evidence suggests that longer hours may actually have the opposite effect because people get too tired to do their best thinking. Your company has a responsibility to clarify what it expects you to produce or provide. Unrealistic performance targets can lead to shortcuts, unsafe practices, number fudging, and other potentially nonproductive activities, especially if you and others feel pressured into making your numbers look good.

If you feel you are on a fast-moving treadmill on a journey that you are not sure is meeting your personal and professional needs, decide now to stop and talk things over with someone you trust. You may need to spend time with your manager discussing priorities and pressures. If you have been a reliable asset to the company, your manager and others will want to help you and keep you as an employee. During these discussions, remember to focus on your personal values and needs so that work fits into your life and not vice versa. Honest and open conversations about ways to balance what you want and what your company needs will help you sharpen your communication skills, help you build your reputation as a valuable contributor to your company's success, and help you create effective relationships with the right people. We will examine these topics in our next chapters.

3

Sharpen Your Communication Skills to Enhance Your Reputation

Half the world is composed of people who have something to say and can't, and the other half who have nothing to say and keep on saying it.

—Robert Frost, American poet

In today's hectic work environment, where time is at a premium and doing things right the first time is essential, learning to communicate for results has become more critical than ever before. Of course, communication problems have always had a costly effect on companies, and there are countless horror stories about missed opportunities, lost business, and wasted efforts. But now, with increased competition and greater demands to do more with less, the stakes are even higher. There is a critical need for you to sharpen your communication skills and establish your reputation as a person who gives and gets information effectively.

A good place to start is by determining the most important information you need to succeed and what information you need to share with others to help them and your company meet current objectives. Ask yourself the following questions about what you need to get from others:

- What information do you need to do your job in a timely and cost-effective way?

- Who has the information you need?
- How do you usually get the information you need?
- How can you get additional information when you need it?
- What can you do to improve the way you get information?

Now ask yourself the following questions:

- What information do you have that will help others do their jobs more effectively?
- Who needs information that you have?
- How do you currently give them this information?
- How can they get additional information when they need it?
- What can you do to improve the way you give them this information?

If you want to achieve or improve your interpersonal effectiveness, you will need to examine your communication efforts with everyone you interact with at work each day. Do not include in your initial analysis relationships or friendships that are an important social part of your work life, but not necessarily essential to the work you are doing. For now, stay focused on those key individuals who have the greatest impact on your ability to achieve your goals and anyone who relies on you for information.

The challenge is to figure out how to achieve open, two-way communication as efficiently as possible. The chart in Figure 3-1 will help you determine strategies for maintaining your successful interactions and techniques for improving ones that are not. Start with the one individual—your manager, a coworker, a customer—who has the most significant effect on your current work activities. Decide how things are going now, determine if you need to make any changes, and schedule time with this individual to discuss what is going well and what could be better. This type of feedback will confirm your interest in developing and maintaining effective interpersonal relationships. If something is working well, letting the other person know will reinforce particular behaviors or techniques that are helpful to you. Telling someone, "Thank you for preparing a few examples ahead of time because it really helped me understand the scope of the problem," will encourage the person to use examples in future conversations with you. If something is not working well, making a suggestion for improvement will help fine-tune your communication efforts. Saying, "I think we rushed through the end of our meeting and did not take enough time to summarize," can set the stage for discussing ways to recap conversations for clarity and completeness.

Once you have tried this "Communicating for Results" checklist

Figure 3-1. Communicating for results.

Name: _____

I. **Giving Information**

   • What do I need to give this person?

   • How do I currently give it?

   • What's working that we should continue doing?

   • Any problems or concerns?

   • Any suggestions for improvement?

II. **Receiving Information**

   • What do I need to get from this person?

   • How do I currently get it?

   • What's working that we should continue doing?

   • Any problems or concerns?

   • Any suggestions for improvement?

III. **Feedback** I want to give this person about our communication efforts:

Scheduled meeting for _____

with the most important person you interact with, repeat the process with others who are critical to your success. Your analysis may help you identify patterns or trends that you can fix yourself or areas in which you can save time and energy by helping others work with you to improve your mutual efforts. If you sense there are problems with your current communication activities and you are not getting the results you need, continue your analysis by examining the process and identifying exactly where breakdowns are occurring.

Start with what happens when you need to request and then receive information from someone else. The following questions can help:

- What is the best way (the fastest, clearest, easiest way) for you to get the information you need?
- What do you need to do to ensure that you get timely, accurate, and complete information—exactly what you need to meet your goals and deliver the required results?
- Do you request specific data, or do you leave room for the other person to decide what or how much information you need?
- Are you clear about your timelines and deadlines?
- Do you let others know they can give you the information you need even if it is "bad news" or difficult feedback?

Being receptive to honest feedback and asking for it on a regular basis will let others know that you are serious about maintaining productive communication with them. If you are having problems with the quality of their interactions with you, you will need to determine the best way to discuss steps you need to take together to strengthen your interpersonal relationships with the key people you depend on for information.

Now look at the opposite side of the process and ask yourself some questions about what happens when you need to *give* information to others:

- Do you plan ahead by deciding what you need to do to ensure that your communication is timely, accurate, and complete?
- Do you determine which facts or examples you can use to ensure that your communication is data-based and objective?
- Do you ask people about their priorities and deadlines?
- Are you honest when you cannot provide the best information or answers in a timely way?
- Do you understand the other person's preferred way of receiving information, and do you respect those preferences?

Keep track of the best way to communicate with coworkers, customers, suppliers, and other key people you interact with on a regular basis. Evaluate what has worked for both of you in the past, and do what you can to replicate successful past practices. A little preparation time will make a big difference in the quality of your communication. Remember that one of your major challenges today is to do things right the first time.

It can be very frustrating when a message is misunderstood, minimized, or ignored. Having to correct these communication problems usually creates additional pressure and can make your follow-up efforts more stressful than they need to be. Having to start over is twice the work. Having to undo previous misunderstandings requires additional time and energy, and you may resent devoting it to an activity you thought was already completed. That is the major reason why you should do everything you can from the beginning to set the stage for success.

While you are thinking of your communication activities, don't forget to analyze the best way—time, place, method—for you to give information to people who are above you in the organization. Start with your manager and review what has worked for the two of you in the past. Focusing on your manager's communication preferences can help you tailor your messages to specific situations. For example, how does your manager want to be informed about real or anticipated problems? Should your initial conversation include your recommendations or should you start with an exploratory discussion outlining your concerns? Are there certain situations in which you have the authority to take action and then let your manager know what you have done? If you are not certain which approach is better or preferred, ask for some direction.

Of course, communicating with your manager may be more difficult than you would like it to be. The following case study provides an example.

❖ ❖ ❖ ❖ ❖

CASE STUDY

Amanda H. is a sales representative for a national food service company. Her boss, Sam, likes to do what he calls "curbside coaching" after they have been out together on an important sales call. He usually pulls into a convenient parking space near the customer's office and asks open questions such as, "How do you think we did?" and "How could I have done better?"

Amanda and Sam just finished a meeting at Ajax International, and Amanda hopes she can get back to her office without being asked for her opinion. She thought that Sam monopolized the conversation, that he didn't really listen to the customer's concerns about delivery delays, and that he launched into a closing statement that covered her part of the meeting. However, Amanda knows Sam is pleased with the way the meeting went.

He even said, "Well, that went well!" when he got into the car. Amanda has a different impression.

Your Analysis

Before reviewing Amanda's approach to this problem, take a few minutes to write down some of your ideas about this situation. What would you do and why?

The Employee's Actions

Amanda decided that if she did not discuss the meeting with Sam, the same behaviors would occur the next time they went on a joint sales call. She decided to approach the subject using Sam's initial invitation—"How do you think we did?"—and stated, "I think we could have done better on the problem of delivery delays. We will probably need to call Ajax to make sure we have addressed all of their concerns. And Sam, I would like to make that call if you don't mind. It was part of our original plan, but I think you were on a roll at the end of the meeting and I did not feel that I made any major contribution." At first, the conversation was difficult, but Amanda believed it set the stage for future discussions about, "How can we get better?"

❖   ❖   ❖   ❖   ❖

More and more organizations today are encouraging managers to share decision-making and problem-solving with their employees. Often called "empowerment," this shift in perspective can give you greater control over your own work and more freedom to be creative when you are resolving problems. If your manager wants you to take more responsibility in dealing with your own work issues, make sure you understand and respond appropriately to this new expectation.

However, this is another one of those areas of change where you will need to balance input and output. Are the results of your problem solving efforts worth the time and energy you are investing? Are you skilled enough to make effective choices with minimal help from others? You probably are, but it may be useful initially to track your time and the results you are actually achieving. Make sure there is an adequate payoff. If you have not had previous experience making decisions or solving problems, you may need to approach this new challenge with cautious enthusiasm. You may need to get support from your manager as you try out the skills and techniques we will present in Chapter Six.

In the past, many companies encouraged employees to park their brains at the front door and depend on someone in management to take care of all their worries and concerns. Breaking away from this type of dependency may not be easy, but it may be necessary in today's fast-paced environments. Make sure you know what your manager expects from you, and then respond with confidence and enthusiasm. Use the skills you have and develop any new ones you need to become a more independent thinker. You can minimize potential risks by practicing on less critical and less complex issues.

Determine the best way to communicate with your manager about critical issues. Then take a look at the way you have been handling your routine communications. How does your manager want to be informed about your day-to-day activities? Review what you do now and decide what has been working so far—face-to-face meetings, written reports, e-mail updates, summaries of interactions with internal or external customers, status reports about your projects and production activities, some combination of all of these, or other communication methods. Then determine if there is room for improvement. Are you giving your manager enough or too much information? Does your manager need weekly reports or can you save time for both of you by shifting to a monthly report? Has e-mail become a comfortable (but perhaps ineffective) way for you to keep in touch with your manager—would an occasional meeting be useful?

By examining your current communication practices, you can fine-tune your efforts to ensure you are being effective and efficient. The self-assessment form in Figure 3-2 will help you get a quick snapshot of your overall strengths and areas for improvement. If you would prefer examining how you did in a particular conversation, the form in Figure 3-3 can help you decide what went well and where you may have missed key opportunities. The payoffs to you in doing these types of self-assessments can be significant. Sharing vital information with others will help confirm your reputation as a team player and will enhance your value to the company.

By practicing communication techniques focused on getting results and meeting your priority goals, you can actually help others sharpen their skills as well. The best way to build your reputation as an effective com-

(text continues on page 60)

Figure 3-2. Communicating for results: self-assessment.

Evaluate your current skill level in the following face-to-face communication activities. Be brutally honest with yourself so that you identify areas where you need or want to invest some personal development time. If it would be helpful, consider asking others for their assessment of your skills:

	One of my best skills	Needs some improvement	Needs much improvement
When giving information or feedback:			
• I make sure the other person is ready to listen.			
• I select the right words and tone of voice.			
• I make a determined effort to be specific and clear.			
• I validate my information or feedback by using recent examples.			
• I check for understanding by asking appropriate questions.			
• I summarize the conversation to make sure there is little chance of misinterpretation.			
• I seek agreement about what actions need to be taken as a result of our conversation.			
When asking for information or feedback:			
• I let others know I am open and receptive to what they have to offer me.			
• I listen carefully, not selectively.			
• I ask clarifying questions to make sure I understand the content of the message.			
• I ask probing questions to make sure I understand any underlying feelings or hidden messages.			
• I resist justifying or defending my behavior if the feedback includes constructive criticism.			
• I paraphrase or restate to make sure I have interpreted the information correctly.			
• I reach agreement with the other person about what actions need to be taken as a result of our conversation.			

Figure 3-3. A self-assessment of specific interaction.

Evaluate your effectiveness during a recent conversation with someone you count on (or someone who counts on you) for information. Depending on the importance of your relationship with this individual and your ability to share honest feedback with one another, you may want to use this checklist to discuss the effectiveness of your current communication efforts.

An Assessment of My Meeting with _____ on _____

	Yes	No	Not Sure
When giving information or feedback:			
• I made sure the other person was ready to listen.			
• I selected the right words and tone of voice.			
• I made a determined effort to be specific and clear.			
• I validated my information or feedback by using recent examples.			
• I checked for understanding by asking appropriate questions.			
• I summarized the conversation to make sure there was little chance of misinterpretation.			
• I sought agreement about what actions needed to be taken as a result of our conversation.			
When asking for information or feedback:			
• I let the other person know I was open and receptive.			
• I listened carefully, not selectively.			
• I asked clarifying questions to make sure I understood the content of the message.			
• I asked probing questions to make sure I understood any underlying feelings or hidden messages.			
• I resisted justifying or defending my behavior if the feedback included constructive criticism.			
• I paraphrased or restated to make sure I had interpreted the information correctly.			
• I reached agreement with the other person about what actions needed to be taken as a result of our conversation.			

municator is to show the people you work with that messages are being transferred successfully, that you all are spending less time fixing past communication breakdowns, and that you are willing to make this vital process work to everyone's benefit.

Of course, there are specific skills that can help you have the impact you want. Although most people recognize the importance of these skills, very few take the time to develop and practice them. There are not many people, for example, who would disagree that listening is a critical competency. Yet think of the countless number of people you meet at work who have not developed this skill, but believe they have. This is an opportunity, therefore, for you to have an edge over others in your daily work activities.

If you make the effort to sharpen your own skills and succeed in making even modest improvements, you will be able to set yourself apart from others who do not take the time or have enough interest to improve. Before considering specific actions you can take, let's look at a broader overview of how the individual components fit together.

Communication has been defined as the process of reaching a "common" understanding with others by sharing your ideas and feelings. When it works, it is the process that moves a thought or concept accurately from one mind to another; it is the successful transfer of meaning from one person to another.

According to reliable research, we spend about seven out of every ten waking hours communicating. We use speech for about 75 percent of that communication. Conservative estimates state that most people speak at a rate of 150 words per minute, or 9,000 words per hour. There are many opportunities, therefore, for messages to get garbled and for our words to lose their full power. Certain types of language have built-in dangers and need to be avoided completely or used carefully. For example:

■ Idioms like "ballpark guess" or "let's cut to the chase" only confuse someone trying to receive your message. If that person is uncomfortable asking for clarification, miscommunication can occur.

■ Euphemisms like "right-sizing" or "voluntary disengagement" weaken language and distort the true meaning of words. Of course, this practice is sometimes an intentional one if a person is trying to "sugarcoat" an uncomfortable message. However, the detour is usually only a temporary one if the receiver has the confidence to ask, "Exactly what do you mean?"

■ Jargon like "a target relocation program" or "modem parameters" may actually alienate a receiver who is trying to keep track of some secret language being used glibly by another person.

■ Acronyms like "WYSIWYG" (computer shorthand for "What you see is what you get") or the classic ASAP ("as soon as possible") can shorten your communication activities, but can also create additional problems for you. Even understanding that you mean "as soon as possible" does not provide the specific time information a person needs to meet your expectations. "By tomorrow afternoon at three o'clock" is much better.

Effective communication is primarily the speaker's responsibility. When you send your ideas to someone, remember that your message needs to be sent in an open, honest, and clear manner so it does not require a great deal of decoding by the receiver. Be alert for any signs that the receiver is confused or has misunderstood your message. Be aware of the nonverbal aspects of communication (body language, gestures, eye contact, appearance, intonation, and facial expressions) to ensure that you are not sending "mixed messages."

Words are the tools we use to convey ideas, feelings, and intentions. Again, it is primarily the speaker's responsibility to choose language that is appropriate and precise for the occasion, easily understood by the receiver, and specific enough to minimize misinterpretation or confusion.

Effective communication also depends on your reputation, credibility, and intentions. The success of today's conversation often depends on whether you have been clear, straightforward, honest, and trustworthy in the past. The receiver of your message may make immediate decisions about whether to trust your motives or question whether you have a hidden agenda. One of the best ways to develop a reputation as someone who is serious and sincere about your communication skills is to analyze how you are doing and discuss any real or potential problems with the individuals you talk with on a regular basis.

In addition to selecting the best words, you need to pay attention to a number of common environmental barriers that can interfere with communication if you do not manage them effectively:

■ *The location of your meeting or conversation is critical.* To ensure that the other person hears the words you have decided to use, pick a place where noises are at a minimum. If your message is confidential or potentially embarrassing, find a place with a degree of privacy where you can limit interruptions and deal with any surprise visitors. You may also want to take a quick look around the area to make sure there are no visual distractions that will hamper your efforts. Several examples come to mind: a particularly active or interesting screen saver on your computer; an especially appealing panoramic view of some beautiful scenery outside the building; a cluttered desk or work area; or some office decoration like the movie poster a colleague of mine once had hanging directly behind his desk showing the bloodied face of Robert DeNiro in *Raging Bull*—quite a distraction.

■ *The time and timing of your conversations can also determine how effective they are.* Be sure to pick a time that is convenient for both parties. Make sure you and the other person can give the interaction adequate time and attention so that neither of you feel hurried. During the conversation, if you feel time is working against you, do what you need to do to adjust or reschedule. Do not cut corners to race through important meetings or you will pay a greater price later. However, if there are unexpected interruptions that are interfering, it may make sense to try again at another time. If the pace of the meeting has slowed down because of any other interpersonal problems—too much detail being shared, too many questions being asked, a sense that key issues are being ignored or minimized, a feeling that there may be too many conflicting agendas or objectives—the best thing may be to step back and discuss what is going on so that adjustments can be made before continuing. You may want to suggest taking a time-out from the content issues of your meeting to examine why the process is not working.

■ *The way you prepare for the conversation and the way you help the other person understand beforehand what you want to discuss can make a big difference.* Being as precise as possible can set things up for success: "Would you be able to spend about fifteen minutes with me before lunch today reviewing our department's latest production goals so that I can make any necessary adjustments to my schedule? If you want me to update you about the status of my current activities, we will need more time, maybe a total of thirty minutes."

Communication is only successful when a message is accurately received. If you take the time to practice and develop two essential skills—listening and asking questions—you will quickly distinguish yourself as a serious communicator. It is obvious that effective listening has many benefits. It lets you know what is going on around you so that you feel more competent and confident. It helps you understand others and win respect from them especially if you handle their messages in a spirit of mutual trust. It helps you to be more understanding and empathetic and diffuse negative emotions in difficult situations.

We all value and respect a good listener, and we can usually explain what makes a person a good listener. We can list the qualities that good listeners practice all the time:

- They concentrate on your message and stay focused on what you have to say. They let you know by their actions that they intend to pay attention to you.

- They use verbal and nonverbal cues to assure you that they are "tuned in" to the conversation. They make excellent eye contact, nod affirmatively, and use encouraging word signals (OK, Uh-huh, Right) to let you know they are keeping up with you.

- They do not interrupt or change the subject. They do not shift emphasis from your story to theirs ("you think you have it bad, let me tell you about my crisis").

- When necessary and appropriate, they ask clarifying or expanding questions to help them understand before they react or respond to your message.

- They paraphrase, restate, or summarize the message to make sure you have reached a common understanding.

If you are interested in improving your listening skills, start by identifying your barriers:

- Are there problems in your environment?
- Are you using your listening time inappropriately by preparing your response, letting your mind wander, jumping to conclusions, reacting emotionally to the message or the speaker?
- Are you letting biases interfere with the way you hear the other person's message?
- Are you tuning out negatives (selective listening) or exaggerating positives (wishful thinking)?

Once you identify the barriers, you can choose from many techniques to improve your listening skills. Some common ones are listed below:

- *Concentrate on the speaker's message.* Stay focused. Try to understand both the content of the message and the speaker's feelings about the message. Most people have difficulty talking clearly about their feelings, so careful attention is necessary. Focus on the content of the message; try not to think about your next statement while the person is talking.

- *Listen for what isn't said.* Avoiding key points or agreeing too quickly may be clues to something the person really wants to discuss. Body language, eye contact, tone of voice, and other cues might be indicators that the other person is reluctant to talk openly. Depending on your relationship, you may want to probe a little—"What else should I know about this problem?" If you feel quite comfortable with the speaker, you might want to simply say, "Let's put all our cards on the table on this one."

■ *Confirm what you have heard.* Restate the message you have received as a way of clarifying words, meanings, and feelings. Sometimes a listener simply serves as a mirror (reflecting what the person has said), to encourage the speaker to continue talking. Occasionally, you may need to make summary responses such as "You believe our new equipment is already obsolete," or "You think the project manager is playing favorites." Keep your tone neutral, and try not to lead the person to your conclusion.

■ *Make sure you understand the message before you respond to it.* Don't make judgments until you know all the facts. Reserve your evaluation or assessment of the message until you are certain you understand it clearly. If the person genuinely wants your viewpoint, be honest in your reply. But while you are listening, try not to express your views in a way that might affect what the other person is trying to say.

■ *Respond to the message in a way that shows you have listened carefully.* When responding, use the other person's own words, key points, and main ideas.

Being an effective listener establishes your credibility with others and encourages them to share important information with you. Demonstrating that you consider listening a serious business sends a message that you care about others and want to take the time to pay attention to what they have to say. Good listening often leads to better relationships based on trust and mutual respect.

Asking questions effectively is the second critical skill you can develop and practice when you receive information or feedback from others. There are several common types of questions that can help clarify the meaning of messages you receive. All of them are useful and have a specific purpose:

1. *Closed questions* require a yes or no answer and are useful to:

■ Establish facts—Did the first shipment leave the plant before the roads got icy?
■ Confirm agreement—So you want me to work exclusively on this project, right?
■ Clarify understanding—Are you saying that this is a higher priority now?

2. *Open questions* encourage the other person to speak more about the topic and are useful to:

- Expand ideas—Why do you think I should try a new approach?
- Seek information—What happens when this project ends?
- Invite participation—How will my suggestion affect the outcome of our work?

3. *Probing questions* go deeper than the words and are useful to:

- Uncover specific details you need—Why do you think that new approach will solve the problem?
- Go beneath the surface of the message to reveal the other person's feelings, beliefs, and rationale—Can you tell me why you are worried about this new procedure?

Good questions can help you clear up misunderstandings during your conversations so that later you are not second-guessing yourself or the other person.

There are only two ways you can develop more open communication channels and improve your working relationships with the people you interact with on a regular basis. Both involve feedback about actions and behaviors that either help or hinder the way you work together. Feedback turns one-way communication into two-way communication. It gives you and the other person a chance to examine *how* you are doing (the process) and *what* you are trying to accomplish (the results).

1. *Receiving feedback.* When you need feedback from others, sometimes they give you what you need without being asked. Sometimes they give you more or less than you want, and you have to clarify what information is most useful to you. Occasionally, however, you will have to ask for feedback so you can get the results you want, repeat or modify certain behaviors, and maintain a high level of performance. These exchanges help eliminate any blind spots you have about what you are doing, how you are doing it, and how you can get better. The information you receive may be practical and useful data that will help you move along successfully toward the accomplishment of your goals. On the other hand, some feedback can help you learn more about yourself and your work habits. When it comes from people who want you to succeed, this type of feedback provides valuable insights into behaviors you may want to stop, start, or continue doing.

2. *Giving feedback to others.* The old saying that "information is power" has taken on a new meaning in corporate America. In the past, the idea was to protect any information that gave you an edge over someone else. Options ranged from withholding data to manipulating it. The more you knew, the more important you were. Today, the pendulum has swung in the opposite direction, and information power is more likely to be measured by your willingness to share what you know. Giving others what they need to accomplish their goals, doing it in the most efficient way possible, and fixing any problems as quickly as you can have become new performance standards in many organizations. Passing along feedback that someone else can use makes good business sense and benefits everyone. Sharing your experiences, ideas, and beliefs can also help others broaden their perspectives and see things in new and different ways. There is an additional benefit you get from sharing information with someone else: The other person has a chance to learn more about you—your background, values, priorities, feelings, opinions.

When you give feedback to someone, especially if it is sensitive or critical information, think about your feedback from the other person's perspective. Focus on what the individual has done or is doing—specific actions and behaviors—and avoid feedback that is based on personality factors, assumptions, or any nonbehaviors.

- To help the other person *understand* your feedback, be specific and accurate. Giving a recent example can help.
- To help the person *accept* your feedback, be descriptive, not judgmental, and allow time to discuss feedback.
- To help the other person *act* on your feedback, discuss the potential consequences if certain actions or behaviors do not improve.

If your current communication efforts do not produce the results you need, you may want to try a different approach. For example, e-mail has become one of the more popular means of communicating with people at work. Electronic messages, however, can be ignored. In some cases, you cannot even be certain the other person has received your message. Therefore, if you need or want an answer quickly, and the other person is not responding, try a more low-tech approach such as a telephone call or a face-to-face meeting.

If, however, you decide that e-mail is your best approach, the following guidelines may be helpful:

- The same rules of grammar apply whether you use e-mail or regular mail. Check your spelling before you send any message.

■ Messages should be brief, usually no more than two or three paragraphs. They should include some form of greeting, even if it is simply, "Ms. Jones," or "Hi Tom."

■ Use accurate subject descriptions—"April 30 Budget Report" or "Revisions to Research Request Form"—so that you and the receivers of your messages can sort, prioritize, and store them effectively.

■ Use asterisks for emphasis. Avoid using all capital letters. It is considered cyber-shouting and rude.

■ Remember, all e-mail messages can be printed out and saved as hard copies, so never say anything on line that you would not say face-to-face.

■ Never write anything in e-mail that you would not want circulated.

■ Check your e-mail a few times each day and respond to messages within twenty-four hours.

■ If you want to forward someone else's message to another person, check with the sender first. Never use the sender's addresses for your own purpose without asking permission. This is the equivalent of using someone's private address book.

■ If you want to give someone permission to forward one of your messages, say so in your message: "If you have found this message useful, please feel free to pass it on."

A colleague recently showed me an e-mail message he received from his supervisor. It read: "WHAT'S GOING ON HERE? I DON'T UNDERSTAND WHY YOU DID THIS. IT'S NOT WHAT I THOUGHT WE AGREED TO DO. I THOUGHT WE AGREED THAT YOU WOULD WORK ON THE *TUSCAN* PROJECT FIRST SO I COULD TAKE THAT INFORMATION TO MY MEETING TOMORROW. LET ME KNOW ASAP WHAT'S GOING ON." Cyber-shouting is just one of their communication problems.

If you have requested feedback from someone, including your manager, and a conversation has not been arranged, you may want to try again by reemphasizing exactly why you have requested the meeting. Sometimes, you can heighten the importance for the other person by stressing some possible consequences—"I need your ideas about this customer's complaint, and I will miss our deadline if we don't resolve this soon."

If you have repeated your message in a different way but you are still not getting results, you need to rephrase your message in more direct, specific language: "We have six more days to complete our budget report, and I need last year's numbers and this year's projections from you by

Thursday. Let me know if that's a problem for you." Once you have re-
framed your message, decide the best way to deliver it, remembering that
a telephone call or in-person approach might work best in this situation.
Putting your message in writing and getting one in reply also adds a degree
of importance and formality to your communications. A memo carries
more weight than the spoken word—it is more official; it can be reviewed
to jog the reader's memory; it can be used to outline specific details of
what has to be done, by when, and by whom. It can also be the document
you and others refer to when agreements or commitments have not been
met and consequences or problems need to be addressed.

You started this chapter by identifying the key people you interact
with on a regular basis, those individuals you depend on to achieve your
goals and priorities. You also identified individuals who depend on you for
information and feedback. Before closing this chapter, take a few minutes
to broaden your perspective about others you need or want to include in
your circle of contacts.

Use the form in Figure 3-4 to list some of the other people you want
to make sure are included in your regular communication activities. As
you develop your list, remember the people you have already identified
including your manager, internal customers, coworkers who depend on
you to do their jobs, a manager in another department where you might
like to work someday, an influential project team leader, or a veteran employee who seems willing to help you develop your skills.

Figure 3-4. Creating a network.

People I want to please	Why	How?
People I want to im-press	Why	How?
People I want to know me better	Why	How?
People I can learn from as mentors or coaches	Why	How?

Then review some of the specific skills and techniques discussed in this chapter and mark those that will help you in your ongoing communication efforts. Use the following checklist as a summary reminder:

- ❒ Keep others informed within my work unit and across departmental lines.
- ❒ Provide quick, logical, and accurate responses to questions and suggestions.
- ❒ Let my manager know about anticipated problems.
- ❒ Be sure my written reports require little change and are ready by stated deadlines.
- ❒ Be sure my spoken communication is clear and well-organized.
- ❒ Ask for and pay attention to feedback from others.
- ❒ Listen actively for content and tone by clarifying, verifying, and restating messages from others.
- ❒ Provide timely, accurate, and honest feedback to others.
- ❒ Use tact in tailoring messages to the appropriate audiences.
- ❒ Respect others when communicating with them so that I do not embarrass them or put them on the defensive.

To be successful in today's fast-paced, rapidly changing work environment, you will need to sharpen your communication skills so that you are giving and getting the vital information you need to succeed and help your organization continue to prosper. Change the way you look at your interpersonal relationships and broaden your perspective about who can help you maintain or improve your current situation. It is probably impossible for you to do your job completely by yourself. More likely than not, you interact daily with different people inside and outside your company. Effective communication skills are the foundation for these relationships and the cornerstone of your efforts to develop productive links with the right people. That is the subject of our next chapter.

4

Develop Productive Relationships With the Right People

You can make more friends in two months by becoming interested in other people than you can in two years by trying to get people interested in you.

—Dale Carnegie

Your personal and professional success often depends on other people. You can only go so far alone; you cannot succeed at work or in life without help from others. If you want to achieve all you are capable of, you must have support from others. One of the best ways for you to be successful is to build relationships with the right people—key individuals who can help you the most and who depend on you for their success.

The concepts of collaboration and teamwork are emphasized today more than ever in corporate America, especially in organizations that are trying to push decision-making and problem-solving down to the lowest possible levels. Many employees are getting opportunities to be both members and leaders of project teams or special task forces. If you are being challenged to move from an individual contributor role to one that involves closer working relationships with others, the techniques for working together presented in this chapter can help you improve your effectiveness and reduce the amount of time you may be wasting in nonproductive or counterproductive activities. The concepts also apply and can be useful if you need to develop effective relationships with internal or external customers.

In the previous chapter, you were encouraged to list the names of people you interact with on a regular basis. The task now is to narrow that list down to a more selective group. Start by identifying the ten most important people you need to develop and maintain productive relationships with to succeed and flourish. You probably thought about many of these individuals at various places in the last chapter. Now narrow down your list to that handful of people who make up what we will call your Circle of Influence (Figure 4-1). Put yourself in the center of this circle and draw connecting arrows to illustrate the primary nature of your interactions with these key people. For example, if your manager is in one of

Figure 4-1. Your Circle of Influence.

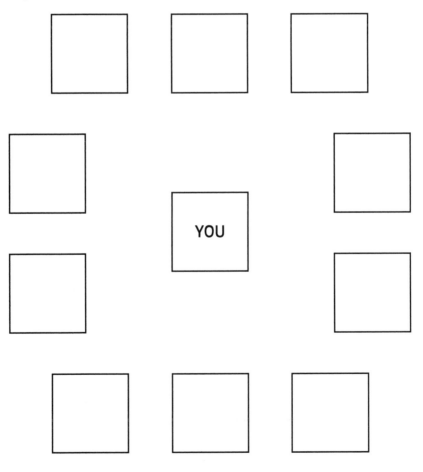

your boxes, one arrow may go out to that box (representing that you give information) and one arrow may come back to you (representing that you also receive information). If a coworker who depends on you for support is in another box, a single arrow may go outward and no arrow come back because you provide information to that person but do not receive any in return. If you have included someone you would like to have as a mentor or coach, and you have not yet approached this individual for help, note a few steps you plan to take to establish a relationship with this person.

When you are creating your Circle of Influence, be careful not to overlook the obvious. Start with your own work group, the people you deal with every day. Don't ignore those relationships that are so routine and habitual that you do not view them as critical to your success. Sometimes these comfortable relationships have the greatest impact on your work efforts. Because they are working so well, however, you may tend to minimize their importance.

Remember those coworkers in your work group who have what experts call "informal power." They are influential because they have years of service, special knowledge or expertise, strategic positions, or associations with key customers. Getting along well with one of your company's twenty-year veterans can help you gain valuable practical information about how your company has done things in the past. Knowing someone who can give you the right technical advice the minute your computer takes an unexpected break can help you stay on schedule with your important deadlines. The names of these key people will not jump out at you from your company's organizational chart. These are the individuals you get to know because you work with them every day or because your paths cross at critical times, on important projects, or when either one of you needs help.

Now consider those people outside your immediate work group. Are there individuals in other areas of the company you depend on a great deal? A colleague recently described the time and effort she spends maintaining an effective working relationship with the manager of her company's purchasing department. There was such a critical need for her to process customer orders in a timely way that regular conversations with the purchasing manager had become a vital part of her job. Most of these interactions were positive and based on what the purchasing department's staff was doing to help my colleague do her job effectively. An occasional "thank you," a box of Valentine candy, or other types of recognition showed appreciation and helped foster a collaborative work relationship.

As you look outside your immediate work area, are there others in your company who affect your work or are affected by what you do? By focusing on the vital links that connect you with others, you can establish an internal network with anyone who helps you determine your priorities and meet your primary performance objectives. Finally, if you are in a position that requires you to make and maintain contacts with individuals outside your organization, your external network may include key people in your profession, your industry, or your marketplace. This last category, of course, includes any external customers you deal with on a regular basis, especially those who are essential to your immediate success. If you deal with customers, do your best to provide quality service and ensure that they are satisfied with your relationships with them. Anticipate and meet their needs while meeting your company's time, quality, and cost requirements. Be comfortable recommending quality solutions to their problems. Be sure your work demonstrates thoughtful insights and technical expertise. Seek feedback on a regular basis about ways you can improve your service to customers.

Once you have identified those key individuals (the "right" people) to devote your time and energy to at work, take a few minutes to determine if there are others (the "wrong" people) who require more of your attention than you can afford to give them. This analysis is not intended to be malicious or mean-spirited. It is meant to be a practical examination of how you spend your time and how you can make sure you are not wasting your efforts. The emphasis should not be on how to end these less important interactions but rather on how to manage them more effectively, especially in ways that may have mutual benefits. For example, see if you can streamline a weekly one-hour meeting with a coworker so that you both get what you need in less time (a half-hour meeting every other week) or in a different way (a pre-meeting written report to focus your meeting time on important issues). Ask yourself if you spend too much telephone time with certain complaining customers at the expense of giving quality time to some of your preferred customers. Decide if certain departments place greater demands on your time without having a corresponding positive impact on your goals and priorities so that you can make some adjustments.

If certain relationships and interactions are out of proportion to their value, it is your responsibility to confront the situation and suggest other options. If you decide not to attempt another alternative, you are tacitly accepting the status quo, and you will need to live with it for a long time or until you reach a point where you cannot take things the way they are anymore. The obvious problem with waiting is that you waste a lot of time along the way, and you may begin to harbor negative feelings and resentment about people who are interfering with your productivity and performance. By the time you finally get around to discussing the problem with them, there may be some strong emotional issues that might not have existed earlier.

This is the problem Andrew faced last year:

❖   ❖   ❖   ❖   ❖

CASE STUDY

Andrew C. and John H. worked together for eight years as cost accountants in a large manufacturing company. They often were assigned to the same project teams, and they needed to share financial data with each other on a weekly, if not daily, basis. Occasionally, they had lunch together or would meet in the break room for a quick cup of coffee on their way to a meeting. During those social times, their conversations were about their families, their hobbies, and John's passion for football.

A major downsizing effort last summer hit the accounting department hard, and several employees who took early retirement were not replaced. The office space was rearranged, and Andrew and John found themselves working in adjacent cubicles. The amount of work increased significantly. Schedules and deadlines were condensed. Pressure to perform more efficiently grew as the accounting department manager scrambled to prioritize assignments and redelegate a mountain of work. Andrew felt the pressure immediately. He put his head down and stayed close to his tasks for nine hours each day. A working lunch in his cubicle became routine, and he convinced himself that things would change once he and his coworkers got control of their new workloads.

In the space next to him, John was also busier than ever. However, a problem began to develop one Monday morning in the fall. Andrew got to work early to plan his day and organize his projects for the week. Ten minutes after Andrew settled in, John walked into Andrew's cubicle and sat on the edge of his coworker's desk. For about twenty minutes, John rambled on about football scores and what he and his family had done over the weekend. After another ten minutes of animated monologue, John announced, "Nice talking to you, buddy, have a good day." By the time this small whirlwind had swept out of his work space, Andrew realized that his best-laid plans had been scuttled. He had lost more than a half-hour of valuable time and actually resented this disruption. John seemed unaware that Andrew was bothered by this lengthy interruption. This was not the first time such intrusions had cost Andrew some valuable preparation time. John did not seem to be getting the hints that Andrew was sending him about needing this early morning time for work issues. Andrew decided the time had come to take a more direct approach to this problem.

Your Analysis

Before reviewing Andrew's approach to this problem, take a few minutes to write down some of your ideas about this situation. What would you do and why?

_____

_____

_____

The Employee's Actions

When Andrew realized that John's disruptive behavior would continue until Andrew confronted him about it, he asked John to take a coffee break with him. Getting away from their cubicles to a more private place was a way to avoid distractions and interruptions, and Andrew could make sure there was adequate opportunity to discuss the feedback he wanted to give his coworker. Andrew wanted to be careful and tactful about this conversation. He knew that he and John would probably be working next to each other for a long time, and he did not want to jeopardize their relationship. For the next fifteen minutes, Andrew talked about how John's early morning conversations had become disruptive to his schedule. He stated clearly the impact these conversations were having on his ability to plan his work for the day and week and how he had to play catch-up afterwards every time. At first John seemed deflated by the feedback, but he listened to his coworker's comments: "I can't afford to take this much time out of the beginning of my day, John. I really enjoy our conversations, but I think we might have to limit them or shift them to lunch or break times. I can't seem to get things done once I've been distracted like that. I need to be able to focus my early morning energy on planning activities."

By the end of their conversation, Andrew and John had agreed on several options that resolved this problem. John agreed to be more sensitive to Andrew's schedule and to be sure he would look for any clues that he was overstaying his welcome. Andrew agreed he would signal to John, "Well, got to get busy here," whenever he started feeling pressure to get down to work. Both coworkers agreed to shift their longer social interactions to break or lunch times.

❖   ❖   ❖   ❖   ❖

If you have a similar situation to deal with, here are a few suggestions that may help:

■ Do not change your behavior to accommodate the other person's actions. The problem will only continue and may get worse.

■ Confront the other person as tactfully as possible by focusing on behaviors and not on the person or on personality issues.

■ Describe the behavior early in the conversation and state the impact it is having on you: "When you walk into my work area and start talking about vacation plans, it interrupts my workflow. This makes me have to stop what I am doing to pay attention to something I may want to hear about, but that is not a priority for me at that time."

■ Suggest an alternative action or behavior that would make things better for both of you: "In the future, I would prefer if you simply let me know what you want to talk about and we can quickly decide what time would be best for both of us. I could stay focused on my current task, and we could pick a better time when I can give your conversation my undivided attention."

■ Get agreement about a workable alternative. Then you can hold each other accountable to honor the agreement you have made.

As you develop your Circle of Influence list, remember that it revolves around you and that others benefit from their relationship with you. Regardless of where you are on your company's organizational chart, you have some degree of influence that comes from several possible sources. For example, your job function itself may put you in a position in which you are a key link in your company's production flow. Others depend on you to keep things moving along and, in turn, you probably depend on a few people to get you what you want when you need it. Your position in the company, therefore, creates a degree of interdependence based on the degree of influence you share with others. As you look at your Circle of Influence, make sure you consider some of those important connections you make with others simply because of your position in the company. There may also be other coworkers you interact with infrequently—a safety expert, a budget expert from the financial department, a corporate lawyer, the manager of your print shop—but their positions make them critical to your success. Some or all of these key people are candidates for your Circle of Influence.

Certain coworkers should make it to your chart of influential people based on the specific knowledge or experience they have that makes them experts in their fields. A computer specialist is a good person to know if your job requires you to keep up with the latest technology. A marketing specialist can be helpful if you need to keep current on demographic trends. A veteran employee can help you understand your company's history and some of the unwritten rules that you may need to know about.

The effectiveness of your Circle of Influence depends on how well you have established and maintained your relationships with the right people. You need to examine, on a regular basis, your list of influential connections to make sure your network of coworkers, customers, managers, and other key people is current and productive. Developing individual contacts with the right people can be an important component of your current and future success.

The challenge is to determine who the right people are, how much time you can afford to spend on your networking activities, and what you can bring to these relationships that will be useful to the other person. Time is such a precious resource that you need to be both honest and selective about building and maintaining relationships. Two questions can help: "How can this person I am in contact with help me be more productive, effective, or efficient?" and "What information, resources, or help can I provide that will make this relationship beneficial to the other person?"

Once you have identified the people you need to devote your time and energy to at work, the next step is to determine the best way to interact with them. Remember that they are individuals, each with his or her own needs, priorities, pressures, and interests. Understanding and respecting their individual differences will help you establish and maintain a good foundation for a successful work relationship. Try to determine what they need or want from you. What are they willing or able to give you to help you do your work? What is the best way for you to work together now so that your future dealings will be positive and productive?

Listening to what others have to say—paying careful attention so that you understand clearly and accurately what is important to them—will provide you with valuable information to help you develop the best kind of relationships. Observing them in action is another way of gaining clues about someone else's preferences and priorities. These insights can provide you with important information about what motivates another person and can help you decide what it will take to build a successful relationship with that individual. The knowledge you accumulate about each key individual in your Circle of Influence can help you tailor your approach and ensure success.

For example, if you work with someone who is analytical and detail-oriented, giving her timely and precise updates on a routine basis may be the best way to let her know that you recognize and respect her needs. She may also be the best person for you to call on when you need facts or figures to support one of your proposed projects. On the other hand, if you work with someone who is more spontaneous and creative, you might find mutual benefit helping each other brainstorm about new approaches to persistent problems. Finally, there are several practices that work for most people—complimenting them for good work, thanking them for helping you on a tough project, sharing important information with them before being asked, soliciting their help in areas where they have experience, expertise, or interest—that go a long way to building and maintaining productive relationships.

Remember that doing your job is not just about getting the work done. It is also about building relationships for the future. Your success will often depend on your ability to influence or persuade others to cooperate with you. One of the best ways to do that is to show that you are genuinely interested in other people—what they are doing, why their activities are important, how you can help. Use your best communication skills: Be a good listener and pay close attention to what they are saying. Ask good clarifying and probing questions to make sure you understand. Encourage people to talk about themselves. Do whatever you can to make them feel important. Remember, you are also interested in discovering what others can do for you. One of the best ways to find out is to learn as much as possible about them. Concentrate on your goal—getting information, support, resources that can help you—rather than on whether or not you like the other person. By focusing on your performance and results, you will be able to minimize or manage any potential personality clashes.

The challenge of developing productive relationships is especially important in organizations that are emphasizing teamwork as their new way of doing business. Companies are now shifting decision-making and problem-solving responsibilities to all levels in the organization. In fact, that is where those activities should have been done all along, where they could have been handled most efficiently. Because of this change in emphasis, you may be getting new opportunities to be a more active member of a project or functional team. For Steve Kauffman, Director of Training and Development at Moyer Packing Company, his company's new approach provided some exciting personal challenges:

> I want to understand the "big picture," not simply be told "get this done." I need to understand my organization's needs. I need to work together with others, to get shared commitment with others, to accomplish things as a team. I need to start with myself: What can I do to make sure I'm being a team player? I need to make sure I'm not being defensive when someone wants to know what I'm doing. I have to have the right motives and set aside my self-centered motives for the good of the team. I need to make sure I'm willing to share credit. I also need to be a good listener so that I understand what others are doing. I need to take the initiative in finding a common ground with the people I'm collaborating with, especially about their priorities and values.

In some cases, you may be asked to participate on special task forces or lead a work team. There are a variety of skills and work behaviors associated with this fairly new approach to getting work done. If you are used to being an individual contributor and not accustomed to collaborating with others, some of the following concepts and practices can be crucial to your success.

There are certain factors and conditions you should know about whenever you are asked to participate on or lead a team. Let's start with a definition of the word "team." In their national bestseller, *The Wisdom of Teams* (HarperBusiness, 1993), Jon R. Katzenbach and Douglas K. Smith present a way of looking at teams that has become widely accepted by many companies: "A team is a small number of people with complementary skills who are committed to a common purpose, performance goals, and approach for which they hold themselves mutually accountable."

There is a growing body of research that supports the value of teams and teamwork in certain situations:

- When there is a significant crisis or problem, individuals often rally around and may even form ad hoc teams to deal with the emergency. Companies that can anticipate these situations create planning teams to develop and implement contingency plans.

■ When a performance challenge is especially complex and involves a wide range of multiple tasks, a team can divide, conquer, and accomplish much more than individuals working separately on specific parts of the problem. There is strong evidence suggesting that the collective strength of a team produces faster response time, better decisions, and more effective problem-solving. Of course, these favorable outcomes depend on how well team members work together and how effectively they use the skills described later in this chapter.

■ When there is a need for innovation, creativity, and different perspectives, a team of people with complementary skills and varied experiences can produce new ideas and approaches that may not have been thought of by one individual or by a group of individuals working independently. This is often referred to as "synergy"—when the efforts and outcomes of the whole team are greater than what any one individual or all the individuals acting on their own could have produced. Effective teams achieve this phenomenon by using team skills like brainstorming, joint problem-solving, and real-time priority analysis. These collaborative actions invite team members to participate, look at new possibilities, remove barriers to their performance, and experiment with different ways to approach situations that often cannot be addressed by doing things "the way we've always done them."

■ There will be occasions when your company and your manager will provide you and other individual contributors opportunities to develop new skills and a broader perspective. Exposure to people with different expertise and approaches can be a beneficial way for you to experience new challenges in your current job. Working on a team can be a unique learning opportunity, which, in turn, can result in higher levels of motivation, enthusiasm, and commitment on your part. Participation on a team can add variety to what may have become a fairly routine job, and it can spice up your week with new and different activities.

If you are currently working on a project team, or if you see being assigned to a team an imminent possibility, find out as much about the project ahead of time so that you can collaborate with others and make a contribution as quickly as possible. Start by understanding your team's purpose or objective. Ask and understand why the team was formed, who formed it, and what outcome you and your team members will be held accountable to produce. This overall objective is often summarized in a management mandate or mission statement that your team should understand and feel committed to accomplish. The team's objective should be something that you and others on your team believe is relevant and worthwhile. The desired outcome should be something you all consider well worth your collective efforts.

Next, be sure you understand your role on the team and your unique responsibilities. Ask yourself, and others if necessary, why you were selected and what you can bring to this endeavor. Are there specific skills you have demonstrated in the past that are being viewed as critical by those who formed this team? Were you tapped to join because you have shown leadership potential or the capacity to be innovative when problems occur? Determining the reasons for your selection can help you understand the role you are expected to play. It is always easier to be accountable when you understand expectations.

Finally, do whatever you can do to help create the right team atmosphere. On effective teams, individual commitment occurs when team members have a feeling of involvement and ownership in the team's activities. Look for and capitalize on opportunities to set goals, solve problems, make decisions, resolve conflicts, and communicate honestly with other team members and the team leader. Although these activities may involve trying out new skills, remember that there may be more experienced people on your team who can help and support you. That is one of the many benefits of teamwork. The right team atmosphere is based on openness, trust, and mutual respect. It requires that team members deal with conflict and disagreements and not eliminate or ignore them. It requires careful attention so that time and energy are not being wasted on counter-productive interpersonal activities. As a member of a team, you share an important responsibility to collaborate with others and to participate fully in team meetings and other project activities.

The ultimate test of a team is its ability to achieve results that individual team members can not accomplish on their own. The diverse talents of the team combine to create an end-product beyond individual capability. Your contribution to these desired outcomes will often depend on how well you practice some of the new work habits described earlier in this book. Your team's success may be tied to your ability to balance multiple demands on your time and resources and meet designated deadlines, schedules, and targeted completion dates. The way you and your teammates interact with each other may depend on how well you have sharpened your communication skills. The pieces all fit together. Chris Rose, Work Control Manager at Vermont Yankee Nuclear Power Corporation, points out several other important components of team work:

> In a work environment that emphasizes teamwork, we all need to understand what's really important. Sometimes what's urgent may not be important. I need to understand the expectations

coming to me and the ones going out from me to others. I need to develop strong relationships with others built on integrity and trust. We are in danger of losing our tribal knowledge. Key people are leaving, retiring. Before they go, we need to understand how they do what they do so that we can pass it on to others.

Here are a few techniques you can use to become a more effective team player:

■ *Share information with others who will benefit from knowing what you know.* If you are not sure whether a piece of information is important, let the other person decide: "I heard some news about one of your customers that I thought you should know," or "Would you be interested in this magazine article I read recently about computer scanners?" Offers like this will establish your reputation as a person who keeps in touch with others about their interests or needs and is willing to pass along information that can be useful to them. Anytime you write a report or document the results of one of your projects, make a list of everyone who might benefit from knowing about your work. You probably have a short list of people who need to know what you have done, but a longer list can include some of your coworkers who might like to know what you have done. Consider circulating reports, customer correspondence, and any other documents that others might find valuable. Giving your associates copies of useful memos, leaving someone a helpful e-mail note, giving one of your colleagues a "heads-up" about a meeting or new company initiative—all of these collaborative efforts demonstrate your willingness to be a team player.

■ *Compliment others for their hard work.* Sometimes a simple "Thank you for getting that information to me so quickly" can make another person's day. Stating your appreciation shows others that you are interested in their work and your relationship with them. Often, because of the pace of our daily lives, we forget to pass on a complimentary word to someone who could use some positive feedback. Sometimes asking a coworker's advice can be a nice way to recognize them for their expertise or their performance—"I know you have made several successful presentations recently, and I was wondering if you would be willing to give me a few tips." Giving coworkers an opportunity to brag a little about their work reinforces your interest in working together in a cooperative atmosphere. It confirms your belief that teamwork is better than competition. A few positive comments can help others around you keep their problems in perspective. You can help maintain a spirit of cooperation and collaboration.

- *Help streamline work processes.* Keep things moving smoothly from your work area to the next. If you see a potential or actual bottleneck, do your best to remove any obstacles that may adversely affect your team's efforts. Get help as quickly as possible. Keep others informed about any pending delays or other problems. Communicate with anyone who needs to know when your part of the work is slowing down or going off track. If you are not going to be able to meet established deadlines, let your supervisor or team leader know immediately. Do not hesitate to ask for suggestions or resources from coworkers who might have a better perspective on ways to improve your work processes. Make sure your continuous improvement efforts include feedback from others.

- *Share credit for your successes with anyone who has helped you.* Letting your superiors know about the contributions others have made to your work projects will reinforce their impression of you as a team player and will strengthen your coworkers' opinion of you as a person who values collaboration. Coworkers will be more willing to work with you, support your efforts, and ask for your help on their projects when you go out of your way to give them credit for their help. Conversely, if a particular task does not go as well as you expected, be willing to accept your share of the blame.

- *Give others data-based information that will help them maintain or improve their current performance.* Careful planning can help you present your views in a way that the receiver will find beneficial. Remember that the other person must understand, accept, and be able to act on your feedback. To make your feedback work, use specific details and examples, talk to people when they are most receptive to hearing from you, allow adequate time to discuss your feedback, and reach agreement about the content of your message. If you frame things in the right language, so that the other person sees the value of your feedback, you will demonstrate that you are interested in maintaining an effective work relationship with them and that you are interested in sharing constructive suggestions about each other's performance. Giving and getting feedback can improve relationships. Sharing your perceptions is the only way you can modify someone else's perceptions of you. If you are tactful and diplomatic, you can keep even your most critical observations constructive and ensure that your honest feedback is appreciated and used.

- *Remember that, within your own work environment, you have the opportunity and ability to collaborate with others in a way that will help you be successful.* To expand your sphere of influence, develop relationships that are built on mutual respect and cooperation. By communicating your willingness to help others succeed, you create a positive work environment and establish a reputation for yourself as a team player.

Most people like to work with someone who is cooperative, helpful, friendly and upbeat. Few people like to work with someone who is cynical, mean-spirited, negative, or disgruntled. Giving people encouragement and positive feedback goes a long way toward establishing a productive, comfortable work environment for everyone. Offering your coworkers information, strategies, support, and solutions that will be mutually beneficial can help establish long-lasting relationships that will make life more productive for everyone.

As you look at your current work situation and the people you interact with on a daily basis, you may decide that you want to change or expand your Circle of Influence. This can happen for a variety of reasons:

- Key people have been promoted or reassigned, and you do not deal with them in the same way as before.

- New internal or external customers have become "preferred customers," replacing others who used to have that status for you.

- You have been assigned to a new project, and the team leader and your fellow team members deserve a different level of commitment and attention from you.

- You have decided to broaden your own sphere of influence and widen your own knowledge base by reaching out to other key individuals in your company.

- You have decided to ask people who are involved in processes or projects you want to know more about to share their information and expertise with you. You have offered to brainstorm with others so that you can share your ideas.

- You have decided to explore opportunities outside your company that will help you learn more about your industry or profession. These activities can be valuable ways for you to exchange information and develop channels of support.

More than ever, building relationships for the future is an important part of doing your job. Remember, however, that your primary responsibility is to get your current work done first. Do not let networking and relationship-building for the future become a substitute for getting your current work done efficiently and effectively.

If you decide to add someone to your Circle of Influence—your list of the "right people"—or if you decide you need to improve your relationship with someone on your list, it can be helpful to examine the rationale behind your decision. The worksheet in Figure 4-2 can help you analyze your motives and expected outcomes. Start with a specific work objective

Figure 4-2. Building productive relationships.

In order for me to accomplish the following work objective,

_____

_____ .

I need to establish or strengthen my working relationship with

_____

_____ .

The benefit to me will be: _____

_____ .

The benefit to the other person will be: _____

_____ .

The benefit to the company will be: _____

_____ .

To establish, maintain, or improve the way I work with this individual, I will have to: _____

_____ .

I think this effort is definitely worth the time, the energy, and the cost it will take.

Yes _____ No _____ Not Sure _____

this person can help you meet, then list as many benefits as you can think of for developing a more productive relationship. Decide which actions you need to take and then determine if the benefits of your efforts outweigh the costs.

Building productive relationships with the right people takes sensitivity and thoughtful attention. Things can get even more complicated when you are competing for fewer resources and working with tighter demands.

Stay focused on whatever mutual benefit each of you can get from the relationship. Be open to their assessment of your performance. Ask for their feedback and listen carefully to their suggestions and ideas. Become comfortable giving them useful feedback that might help them improve their work. Sometimes these interactions are difficult, and you have to remind yourself how important they really are.

Sometimes you may disagree with the other person and find yourself at opposite ends of an argument. If you have already taken pains to build a relationship with the other individual, resolving a conflict can be easier than if you are starting from scratch. If you have even a short history with the other person, there may be some common ground on which you can build a successful resolution to your current difference of opinion. The important thing to remember is that conflict is inevitable. The more you interact with people in diverse work environments, the more you respect their individual differences, the more you welcome new ideas and opinions, the more likely you are to find that you do not agree with someone. In the past, you might have been tempted to ignore or minimize these conflicts. That kind of behavior has become less acceptable in today's organizations, where there is a greater emphasis than ever on finding collaborative win/win solutions to interpersonal conflicts. The next chapter describes some techniques and work habits that will help you take a problem-solving approach to resolve conflicts and stay focused on the problem and not personalities, so that you can get to a mutually satisfying outcome.

5

Use a Problem-Centered Approach to Resolve Conflicts

Don't be afraid to take a big step when one is indicated. You can't cross a chasm in two small steps.

—David Lloyd George

The word conflict comes from the Latin *conflictus* meaning "a striking together." Dictionary definitions usually include descriptors like collision, disagreement, opposition, antagonism, and differences of interests, principles, or opinions. Conflict often stems from initial perceptions: What you perceive as beneficial or useful may appear to be incompatible with the interests or intentions of someone else. As you each attempt to structure the future in different ways, conflict is sure to occur.

Conflict is often viewed as a competition or contest to be won, which automatically means that someone else has to lose (lose power, lose influence, or lose face). It is often viewed as troublesome, negative, and stressful. As a result, many people try to avoid, ignore, or minimize conflict and the issues that cause it. In fact, conflict may or may not involve stress or negative emotions, but there is always the potential that strong feelings exist and will surface. Because conflict is an inevitable element in human and organizational life, learning how to deal with it effectively can set you apart from others who have learned to live with bad situations or made things worse by reacting emotionally to them.

When it occurs, conflict is confusion, disagreement, or resistance that, if not resolved properly, can diminish individual, team, and organizational effectiveness.

Conflict can be a byproduct of working with others. It can happen anytime you want to advance an idea or recommend a new program or approach. You will usually encounter some type of resistance, some differences of opinion, some other perspectives about how, when, and why to proceed. In and of itself, conflict does not have to be negative, disruptive, or counterproductive. It is a natural occurrence you must recognize and confront effectively so that it improves cooperation and teamwork rather than create unhealthy tension or unnecessary disagreements.

In today's fast-paced workplace, there are many sources and opportunities for conflict. Here are a few of the most common ones:

- *Reactions to Change.* Some people have significant negative responses to trying something new. They prefer to hold on to old approaches, "the way we've always done things around here," and drag their heels even when talking about another way. They may have strong emotional reactions—sadness, fear, anger—to any type of change. They usually take one of the options described in the Introduction to this book—Fight, Flight, or Freeze.

On the other hand, some people have very positive responses to change. They take that fourth option—Flourish—also described in the Introduction. They look for opportunities and try to focus on the positives in the changing situation. They get excited by the potential good that can come from innovation and new approaches.

These different perspectives about change can cause conflict, which, if handled effectively, can provide opportunities for healthy and helpful discussions.

- *Competition for Limited Resources.* As organizations tighten their financial belts and reorganize to become "leaner and meaner," there will be fewer people, less money, and greater demands on equipment and materials. The opportunity for conflict is unavoidable as you try to negotiate with others for the resources you need to be successful.

- *Different Goals or Priorities.* Few things can be more frustrating or conflict-producing than learning that one of your highest priorities is actually very low on someone else's list. A colleague recently described a situation in which she needed to mail out new marketing brochures to all of her customers by the end of April. Although she was fairly certain she had discussed this project with the print shop manager in January, she was surprised to learn that it had become a midsummer project for him and his work team. Their initial conversation had some emotionally charged moments that they needed to work through or the conflict could have gotten out of control. We'll review the actual outcome of this situation in a case study later in this chapter.

■ *Communication Breakdowns.* Conflict can occur when you think you have communicated effectively with another person but find out later that you did not achieve a common understanding. Your expectations were not clear. Your priorities were misunderstood. Your understanding of your role on a project was different from someone else's. These differences of opinion need to be addressed and resolved constructively so that they do not continue to adversely affect your relationship with the people you need to work with every day.

Celestine Mack, Customer Service Consultant with SmithKline Beecham Pharmaceuticals, believes that dealing with conflict is always a risk.

> We can never be sure how the other person will respond. But I went to a vice president and explained that something he said offended me. I said, "Can you help me? I would like to understand what you meant by that comment." Usually, when I confront the issue, I find the rewards outweigh the risks. I speak my mind in a way that is professional. I deal with things in a positive manner by staying focused on the things I can control.
> Conflict is healthy for me. If something is bothering me, I cannot walk away. I tell people, "If I have done something to hurt you, please come talk to me." That's people-friendly, positive, constructive. If I have a conflict with someone, I go to them and say, "You hurt my feelings when you made that comment" or "Is there something we can do to work through this problem?" It is important to get to a resolution.

❖ ❖ ❖ ❖ ❖

CASE STUDY

Karen D., an investment advertiser, had several important communication goals to achieve this year. Her number one priority was to mail out new marketing brochures to 1,600 customers by the end of April. As mentioned earlier in the "Different Goals or Priorities" section of this chapter, Karen had a major miscommunication problem with Bud S., the print shop manager. In late February, when Karen began asking Bud for a status update about the project, he seemed to brush her question aside by saying, "It's third on my list, and we still have plenty of time." Two weeks later, when Karen asked to see samples of the final product, Bud promised to have one ready for her by the following Friday. When Karen expressed her growing concern, Bud reminded her that he had other projects, priorities, and people to take care of before her. He promised to get to her project as quickly as he could. Four days later, he called to tell Karen that her printing project had suddenly become a midsummer priority for him. Executive management had requested that he give immediate attention to a critical stockholder's report, a revised employee compensation booklet, and a seventy-page prospectus about a new company acquisition. Bud apologized. Karen said, "How could this happen?" and began to panic about how to handle what had just become a major crisis for her.

Your Analysis

Before reviewing Karen's approach to this problem, take a few minutes to write down some of your ideas about this situation. What would you do and why?

_____

_____

_____

The Employee's Actions

Karen told Bud that they needed to meet as soon as possible, but she needed to calm down before she could even talk about this problem. They agreed to have lunch, and Karen came prepared with a short list of questions. Before they got down to the major issue, Karen reassured Bud that she understood how his priorities had been changed by others in the company and acknowledged that those kinds of things had happened to her and others before. Karen assured Bud that she was not blaming him for the situation, but she also emphasized that it had become a real crisis for her. She then changed the focus on their conversation by asking several pointed questions about actions they could take:

- Are any of the marketing brochures completed?
- Is there a way to break down that major printing job into

smaller runs that could be worked in around your other projects?
- If I found some budget money to pay for overtime, would some of your team be willing to put in some extra hours?
- Could we send the project to an outside vendor? That would be my last resort because I know I would lose the quality you have always provided me and the control I need to meet my deadline.
- Are there any other options we should explore?
- Who needs to know about this problem? How and when do we tell them?

At the beginning of the conversation, Bud was embarrassed about what had happened. Karen was still angry and worried. However, they were able to put the emotional aspects aside and move quickly into a problem-centered approach. There were three major outcomes of this conversation:

1. They developed an action plan that included several different options to help Karen close to meeting her schedule.
2. They agreed to communicate more effectively in the future, especially if either one of them anticipated a problem.
3. They agreed they were glad they had talked because working together had always been and would continue to be important for each of them.

❖ ❖ ❖ ❖ ❖

Occasionally, there are other factors that can make dealing with real or potential conflict even more challenging. For example, if you have had previous personality clashes with the other person, you need to understand why these disagreements have occurred so that you can focus instead on the real issues to be addressed. Are your styles different? Are you a status threat to each other? Do you have significantly different values? Do you trust each other? We will look at some techniques to help you do this later in the chapter. Remember that conflict can be an opportunity for new ideas and better rapport. The challenge is to stay as objective as possible so that you can discover, with the other person, a mutually acceptable resolution.

Because conflict is inevitable, you need to be able to decide, as quickly as possible, how you want to deal with it. There are essentially three approaches you can take when you are in conflict with someone else:

1. An assertive approach in which you attempt to push forward your preferred solution to the conflict because you seriously believe it is the best or only alternative. Carried to an extreme, you may run the risk of trying to dominate or overwhelm the other person. You need to be careful that your approach does not become too aggressive or competitive.
2. An acquiescent or passive approach in which you give in to the other person, or minimize your own interests, or ignore the situation completely.
3. A logical, problem-centered approach in which you focus on the issue, its importance, and its impact.

You need to analyze both the rational and emotional components of conflict, then select the approach that will produce the best results for you, for others, and for your organization.

Let's start with the factual, rational side of a conflict you have had or one that you have resolved recently. Use the following action steps and the chart in Figure 5-1 to help you describe your perceptions of the situation.

Step 1: Describe the conflict as briefly and as specifically as possible.

- With whom are you having this conflict?
- When did it start?
- What caused the conflict to start in the first place? Was there a particular incident that triggered bad feelings between you and the other person?
- Has the conflict gotten better or worse since it first began?

Step 2: Describe the impact the conflict is having on your ability to achieve your work goals.

- Is the conflict interfering with the quantity of your work? Are your work efforts being hampered by a lack of cooperation from the other person?
- Would the quality of your work improve if you were able to collaborate with this individual?
- Are you wasting valuable time trying to work around this situation?
- Are there any nonproductive or counterproductive activities that would stop by resolving this conflict?
- What specific costs can you identify that are associated with this conflict? Try to quantify factors like losing time, having to fix mistakes, putting in unnecessary overtime, and any other tangible mea-

Figure 5-1. Action steps: analyzing the situation.

Describe the conflict as briefly and as specifically as possible.

```
┌─────────────────────────────────────────────────┐
│                                                   │
│                                                   │
│                                                   │
│                                                   │
└─────────────────────────────────────────────────┘
```

Describe the impact the conflict is having on your ability to achieve your work goals.

```
┌─────────────────────────────────────────────────┐
│                                                   │
│                                                   │
│                                                   │
│                                                   │
└─────────────────────────────────────────────────┘
```

Describe any broader impact you know this conflict is having.

```
┌─────────────────────────────────────────────────┐
│                                                   │
│                                                   │
│                                                   │
│                                                   │
└─────────────────────────────────────────────────┘
```

Describe the benefits of resolving this conflict.

```
┌─────────────────────────────────────────────────┐
│                                                   │
│                                                   │
│                                                   │
│                                                   │
└─────────────────────────────────────────────────┘
```

sures you can use to determine the impact this conflict is having on you.

Step 3: Describe any broader impact you know this conflict is having.

- Is the conflict affecting others in your immediate work area? Has the morale of the group you work with declined? If the conflict has had an impact on your performance, have others felt the effects?

- Is the conflict affecting others outside of your own work area? Is it making it more difficult for you to work with other departments or work groups?
- Is the conflict affecting the level of service you provide to your customers? Are you cutting corners or compromising your own high performance standards because of this conflict? Are customers complaining?
- Is the conflict causing serious damage to your future relationship with this individual? Does the conflict have the potential to destroy the level of trust and respect you need to work effectively with this person?

Step 4: Describe the benefits of resolving this conflict.

- Would resolving this conflict improve productivity, efficiency, or effectiveness for you, the other person, your department, or the company? How would you be able to measure the improvement?
- Would resolving this conflict help you and others save time and reduce costs? What quantifiable indicators, like reduced overtime or fewer mistakes, would you use to document improvement?
- Would resolving this conflict improve morale in your work group? Would it improve your morale? Would the other person feel better, too?
- Would resolving this conflict improve your current or future working relationship with this individual? Would a productive outcome to this situation help you reestablish credibility and trust? Would a satisfactory resolution at least allow you to achieve a level of cordial cooperation with this person?
- What would be the best resolution for you at this time?

Once you have analyzed the situation, you should have a thorough understanding of the nature, extent, and complexity of the conflict. Remember that this is your perspective and the other person may disagree with some of your conclusions. However, what you should have uncovered, as a result of this brief exercise, is objective, factual data that can help you determine how to approach this particular conflict. The following checklist will help you summarize your conclusions so far and will give you a quick assessment of your options:

- How important is this issue?
  - ❏ Critical   ❏ Very Important   ❏ Marginally Important

- How important is it for you to resolve?
  - ❐ Crucial   ❐ Useful   ❐ Marginally Important
- How much time are you willing to spend resolving this issue?
  - ❐ As much as it takes   ❐ Some   ❐ Little
- How much time are you wasting on unproductive or counterproductive activities?
  - ❐ Too much   ❐ Some   ❐ Little
- How much negative impact is this conflict having on your relationship with the other person?
  - ❐ Serious   ❐ Moderate   ❐ Minimal
- How much value do you attribute to resolving this conflict?
  - ❐ Great   ❐ Significant   ❐ Some

This analysis of the situation should give you the information you need to take a problem-centered approach to resolving this conflict. You should be prepared to determine your next steps. Let's look at the three most common options.

1. Option One is an *assertive* approach based on your decision that this problem or issue is important, that it is impacting your productivity, that it is taking up an inordinate amount of your time, and that it would be better for you and others to resolve this conflict. It is up to you to do something about the problem even though the other person may also be ready to deal with it. Part of your analysis has led you to the conclusion that you need to initiate some action and begin working toward a resolution of the problem. A logical next step is a meeting or conversation with the other person. Before making arrangements for this face-to-face interaction, step back and determine exactly how assertive you need to be. You probably do not want or need to become too aggressive or competitive, so some planning can help you keep things in perspective as you start your conversation. Here are several techniques that can help if you decide to take this approach:

- Determine in advance the exact words you want to say to start the meeting. Make sure you stay focused on the issue and its impact, not on personalities, assumptions, or feelings. Your words should capture the significance of the problem and your commitment to help resolve it. Use the data you collected earlier to reinforce the effects this problem is having on your performance. Practice your opening words, either alone or with someone who can help you fine-tune your approach, and make sure you have covered the key points you want to make.

> At the beginning of this project, when we set deadlines, you agreed that the dates were reasonable. Despite that, twice in the last thirty days, September 12 and again on October 8, you have missed these deadlines and been at least two days late with your reports. Because of these delays, our department is having a difficult time meeting our own target dates. Do you have any suggestions about what we can do to help you meet your deadlines?

- Be sure you are prepared to use "I" statements to describe your assessment of the situation. By taking ownership of your message, you make it clear to the other person that although the problem may be having a broader impact, the purpose of this conversation is to discuss the effect it is having on you. It also reinforces the notion that you are about to present your perspective about the situation and that you are willing to acknowledge there is another side you are willing to hear.

> I'm sure there is an explanation for the missed deadlines, but I need to know how to prevent future delays.

- When you are ready to turn the conversation over to the other person, ask a safe, nonthreatening question that invites participation in the discussion. Let the person know you are open and receptive to a reaction to what you have said so far and that you welcome an opportunity for two-way communication about this problem. Instead of guessing how the other person feels about what you have said, ask a straightforward question to open the door to a productive exchange of ideas.
Examples:

> "So what do you think about what I've said?"
> "How do you see this issue, and what do you think we can do to resolve it?"

> These techniques can help you to convince the other person that you are serious about this important situation and that you need to have it resolved. An assertive approach lets people know you want to deal with interpersonal conflicts as quickly and as effectively as possible. You can establish a reputation for

yourself as a person who confronts important issues honestly and directly. You do not sweep things under the rug. You go to the people you are having problems with instead of talking behind their backs to others. You do not allow problems between yourself and others to simmer or get so bad that they have a permanent negative effect on your relationship.

In the right situations, an assertive approach increases your ability to influence others and work with them more effectively in the future. People know you will stay focused on business issues and concentrate your efforts on work-related solutions. They will know and appreciate that interactions with you will be based on thoughtful preparation and that they will be handled professionally and respectfully. Being assertive may not be the best way to make friends or improve your current friendships. At first, some people may not like the fact that you are taking this direct approach with them. However, once they see the benefits of resolving the conflict they are having with you, they will respect you for what you have done. This can become the foundation for a more productive relationship. Again, one of your key objectives is to help create a successful working environment in which you are able to deal with interference and get the results your organization expects from you.

2. Option Two in dealing with conflict is a *cooperative* approach in which you give in to the other person, minimize your own interests, or decide to ignore the situation completely. This passive or acquiescent reaction to the conflict must be based on your earlier assessment of the situation so that your decision to take a less assertive approach is based on accurate conclusions.

- This conflict is not as important as other things going on in your work world at this time. You know that if it becomes more important or starts to have a bigger effect on your productivity or performance, you will deal with it more directly. For now, you can live with the situation and at least coexist peacefully with the other person.
- You do not have the time to deal with this issue right now, and it is not having a significant impact on your time. Although there may be a strain in your relationship with the other person, as far as you can tell, it is not causing counterproductive or nonproductive activities. You can afford to put this issue aside for a while, keep an

eye on it, and decide later whether it has become a more important priority. For now, "wait and see" is an acceptable approach.

- The other person is not ready to resolve the conflict. There may be too many other priorities or pressures that would interfere with the successful resolution of this problem. As a courtesy, and one that the other person would probably appreciate, you can afford to wait until a better time, especially if the problem is not having a significant negative impact on your performance. Your decision to maintain harmony and not risk disrupting your work environment can establish a stronger foundation for you to work with the other person when the time is right to resolve the conflict.

There are several cautions to consider if you decide to take a cooperative approach to conflict and several techniques you can use to ensure that the other person does not misunderstand your motives or intentions:

- State your position clearly and see if the other person agrees with your assessment of the situation.
  Examples:

  > "Joe, I know you and I need to reach an agreement about how to handle this backlog of requisitions. It's not a real priority for me right now, though, and I was wondering if we could put if off for a few weeks. What do you think?"
  >
  > "Mary, what impact is the new training schedule having on your current deadlines? It seems as though you have been working hard to meet your commitments. Would you prefer postponing our discussion of this situation until things quiet down for you?"

- If you have decided that avoiding this conflict is the best way to deal with it at this time, you may want to let the other person know the reason for your decision.
  Examples:

  > "Elizabeth, I hope you don't think I'm avoiding you or the problem that came up last week. All of a sudden, I have found myself buried under a pile of new crises that need my immediate attention. Can we agree to keep an eye on our situation for now and get together about it if it becomes more troublesome to either of us?"
  >
  > "Marti, I know we need to resolve this problem before it gets out of hand. I think we both need to gather more

information about what is actually causing these occasional flare-ups between us. What do you think? Can we take some time to back off, analyze what's going on, and then schedule time to hash out a solution?"

- If you have decided that the issue is not significant enough for you to worry about, and that you can live with whatever the other person wants to do, make it clear that you have accepted a resolution that works for you.
  Examples:

  > "Rico, now that I have heard your suggestions, I think you have come up with a solution that will solve the problem. Let's try it, and see how things work out."

  > "Elena, that sounds like a great idea, and it certainly is an approach that I am willing to support. Let me know if there is anything I can do to help."

In the right situations, a cooperative approach increases your ability to manage your own time more efficiently so that you are not getting pulled into situations that are less important than other priorities. By determining which problems are most critical and most urgent, you can control where you want to invest your time and energy. By picking your battles carefully, you stay in charge of your performance and priorities. You avoid going to the mat for the wrong reasons. You avoid minimizing critical issues because you are tied up with less significant ones. You avoid trying to deal with every issue that comes along with the same level of attention and energy, and you are able to separate things that really matter from things that might not make a difference.

3. Option Three in dealing with conflict is a *collaborative* approach based on your decision that this is a problem that needs to be addressed as quickly and as effectively as possible. Part of your analysis of the situation has also led you to the conclusion that you will take both an assertive and a cooperative approach with the other person. You need to be firm about certain conditions that are important to you, and you need to be open and cooperative about the other person's interests and desired outcomes. By identifying areas in which you are willing to compromise—your negotiables and your nonnegotiables—you can focus on the facts to make logical, data-based decisions on how to proceed. This problem-centered approach to resolving conflict can help you minimize the emotional aspects of the situation and allow you to emphasize the right things in your problem-solving efforts.

Most conflicts can be resolved effectively if you approach the other person in a spirit of cooperation and collaboration. The following techniques can often bring mutually satisfactory results:

- Describe the problem as you see it. Explain what is happening in your own words. Use specific, recent examples to clarify your interpretation of the situation:

    "The deadline for our project is approaching quickly. What can I do to help you finalize the report before the end of this week?"

- Explain the impact the problem is having on your performance. Let the other person know that the situation is serious enough for the two of you to address and resolve it. Use specific examples:

    "I'm missing important deadlines," "We are running over budget," "Our production level is down."

- Ask for and listen to the other person's perspective. Try to focus on the big picture before attempting to resolve the problem. Be willing to understand the other person's pressures or priorities. Try to uncover reasons for the problem and what the other person needs or wants to make the situation better. Reach agreement about the nature, scope, and urgency of the problem. Determining exactly what is happening and understanding why are the best ways to begin identifying an appropriate long-term solution.

- Agree on the problem and its root causes. By asking good probing and clarifying questions, you can arrive at a solid understanding about what has to happen next. Workable solutions often emerge from collaborative conversations, especially if they are based on mutual respect and stay focused on the problem, not on personalities. You and the other person may discover a win/win solution that incorporates the best ideas of both of you.

- Identify and prioritize possible solutions. List as many alternatives as you can. Be open-minded and as nonjudgmental as possible. By objectively examining as many "what if we did this" options, you and the other person should be able to identify a few workable solutions from which a best one can be selected.

- Once you have determined the best alternative, implement and monitor your solution. Agree on an action plan that includes ways for you to measure progress and recognize success. The only way to know if the problem has been completely resolved is to follow up with each other periodically. Decide what is the best way to keep in touch with each other so that you both can evaluate whether the conflict has been resolved to your mutual satisfaction.

In some cases, you may not be able to invest enough time and energy to reach true collaboration. You may need to resort to compromise as a temporary alternative. Compromise often lets you arrive at a satisfactory outcome and save time. Compromise can reduce conflict without actually resolving it. You give up some of your preferences (your negotiables) in order to get others that are more important (your nonnegotiables). You behave in a moderately assertive and moderately cooperative way. "Give a little—get a little" becomes an effective strategy that can provide a workable solution in several situations—when you are operating under a tight deadline or when the issues are too complex to be addressed in a timely manner.

When you take a collaborative approach to resolving a conflict, you are admitting that you and the other person both have valuable experience, expertise, and insights about the situation. You are willing to discuss alternatives openly. You are willing to consider options in a broader context—what is best for the team, the department, or the company. You are prepared to use objective criteria to evaluate multiple options and solutions. Often called a win/win approach, collaborating is the ideal objective. It is the one, however, that takes the most patience, persistence, and commitment to achieve.

Collaboration can bring you and others many benefits. For example:

- It can establish interdependence. It can be nonthreatening. When people recognize the value of giving or getting help and realize it is expected, they will work together with you to reach common goals.
- It can build commitment, ownership, and morale. People can see the results of their work and share credit for each other's accomplishments.
- It can set the stage for future performance. Productivity can improve when people learn from past mistakes, celebrate their current successes, and modify outdated procedures in response to changing conditions.

Remember these action steps whenever you decide to take a problem-solving approach to resolving a conflict. You can use the worksheet in Figure 5-2 to prepare for your meeting and record any outcomes or conclusions.

1. Analyze the situation and summarize reasons why you believe the problem is serious enough to address.

Figure 5-2. Action steps: resolving the conflict.

Summarize reasons why you believe the problem is serious
enough to address.

```
┌─────────────────────────────────────────────────────┐
│                                                       │
│                                                       │
│                                                       │
│                                                       │
└─────────────────────────────────────────────────────┘
```

Decide what is the best way to approach the other person. Try to
anticipate both areas of resistance and cooperation.

```
┌─────────────────────────────────────────────────────┐
│                                                       │
│                                                       │
│                                                       │
│                                                       │
└─────────────────────────────────────────────────────┘
```

Meet privately with the other person and allow time for a thorough discussion of the issue.

```
┌─────────────────────────────────────────────────────┐
│                                                       │
│                                                       │
│                                                       │
│                                                       │
└─────────────────────────────────────────────────────┘
```

After the meeting, try your approach and review the outcomes.
Agree to meet again in the near future to discuss the ongoing
results of your problem-centered approach.

```
┌─────────────────────────────────────────────────────┐
│                                                       │
│                                                       │
│                                                       │
└─────────────────────────────────────────────────────┘
```

- How important is the issue and your need to resolve it?
- What is the value to you or others if you resolve this conflict?
- What impact is the conflict having on your performance and productivity?
- What is your relationship with the other person?
- What impact is this conflict having on that relationship?
- Are you wasting time and energy because of this conflict?

2. Decide what is the best way to approach the other person. Try to anticipate both areas of resistance and cooperation.

- Will you use an approach that is more assertive than you would usually take because you need to be firm about your needs and desired outcomes?
- Will you be able to take a more cooperative approach because of the nature and significance of the issue and the other person's willingness to resolve it?
- Will you want to use a collaborative, balanced approach focused on working together with the other person to achieve a more effective long-term outcome?
- How much time are you willing or able to spend on this issue?
- How do you think the other person will deal with this situation?

3. Meet privately with the other person and allow enough time for a thorough discussion of the issue.

- Define the problem objectively and nonjudgmentally. Focus on those data-based performance factors—quantity, quality, time, cost—that have convinced you this issue is important enough to address.
- Clarify your position by stating what you need, the nonnegotiables you have identified in your pre-meeting analysis.
- Listen carefully to check your understanding of the problem and the other person's assessment of it.
- Ask clarifying questions to confirm your understanding of the situation.
- Resist offering your opinion of the possible causes of the problem until you clearly understand the other person's perspective.
- Use data and specific examples to help the other person understand your position.
- Consider the broader picture by discussing the impact this conflict will have if it is not resolved effectively.

- Identify as many solutions as possible to resolve the conflict.
- Select the best alternative, and make sure you and the other person are both willing to try this solution.
- Agree on the best way to monitor, evaluate, and maintain a positive solution.

4. After the meeting, implement the proposed resolution and review the outcomes. Agree to meet again in the near future to discuss the ongoing results of your problem-centered approach.

- What did you gain or lose?
- What do you think you will gain or lose in the future?
- What did the other person gain or lose?
- What do you think the other person will gain or lose in the future?
- How do you both feel about these outcomes?
- Were the benefits of your discussion worth the effort?
- What improvements can you point to at this time?
- What have you learned from this experience that can help you in the future?

Remember that all your work relationships have two sides. You have your needs, interests, and priorities—but so does the other person. In your day-to-day interactions with others, it is very likely you will find differences of opinion and opposing viewpoints about the best way to accomplish your desired outcomes. Assertive behavior can help you get what you want; cooperative behavior can ensure that the other person's needs are being met as well. When you balance both types of behavior and take a collaborative approach, you are able to reduce stress, resolve disagreements fairly, and arrive at win/win resolutions to the most difficult conflicts.

In addition to resolving your current conflict, there are several other benefits you gain from the collaborative problem-centered approach:

- Every time you practice these skills, you become better at using them in future situations. You build a level of comfort and confidence in this type of problem-centered activity.

- You establish a reputation as a problem-solver, a person who is willing to take an objective, data-based approach to even the most difficult and awkward situations.

- By finding areas of mutual interest or agreement, you set the stage for other interactions with this person. Your relationship improves, and you are better prepared to address future issues and problems if they occur. You discover common ground that can only improve your level of trust and cooperation.

■ By fostering a give-and-take approach, you demonstrate your strong commitment to open, two-way communication about anything that might interfere with your goals and priorities. You also invite others to approach you when you are preventing them from meeting their objectives.

■ You can identify ways you need to change your own behavior to improve a situation or a relationship, especially if you learn that something you are doing is inappropriate, ineffective, or counterproductive.

■ When you listen carefully to others and respond sincerely to their feedback, you can find new ways to do a better job and get the results you want.

Conflict is not necessarily bad. If it is dealt with openly and honestly, it has the potential for positive outcomes. If you take a problem-centered approach to conflict, you can:

■ Analyze and emphasize important problems, issues, and concerns.
■ Identify new information, solutions, or approaches.
■ Improve interpersonal relationships by creating a higher level of communication, cooperation, and innovation.
■ Generate multiple solutions beyond the two options usually proposed initially when two people are in conflict with each other.

Conflict can also have negative outcomes, especially if ignored, minimized, or viewed as an emotional encounter and not as a logical opportunity for improvement. If you do not take a problem-centered approach to conflict, you may actually:

■ Push yourself farther apart from others. The situation can get worse, and the gap between you and the other person can increase.
■ Perpetuate a climate of distrust and suspicion.
■ Create higher levels of tension and stress. There is resistance and resentment rather than cooperation and teamwork.
■ Reinforce avoidance behaviors in future interactions.
■ Foster lack of cooperation on future projects or in subsequent discussions.
■ Drag others into the conflict to support your side of the situation—a major time-waster for everyone.

- Settle for some watered-down option that does not solve the problem.
- Reduce your productivity and diminish your current level of performance.
- Cause dissatisfaction and lower morale for you and others in your work group.

Remember, it is easier to work *with* people than it is to work *against* them. Think of the hours of time and energy you may have wasted in the past on unnecessary disagreements or pointless conflicts. By not dealing with certain situations, you may be harming yourself and the other person involved, especially if you waste time complaining about the problem without resolving it or let the conflict interfere with your performance.

If you are willing to be both assertive and cooperative in your dealings with others, you can reach collaborative solutions that have long-lasting benefits to everyone involved. Conflict does not have to be negative or disabling. If you are open to new ideas and willing to collaborate with others, conflict can broaden your perspective and present possibilities you may never have thought about before.

6

Take Charge of Your Job: Fix Your Own Problems

A problem well stated is a problem half solved.
—Charles F. Kettering, American inventor

More and more companies are pushing problem-solving and decision-making down to the lowest possible levels of the organization. The idea of empowerment has received widespread attention but limited application. Inviting people to play a more active role in resolving problems is a wonderful idea that can be motivating, challenging, and rewarding to most people. However, if you do not have the necessary skills or if you have never been encouraged to do this before, you may perceive this practice as management abdication (not delegation), an attempt by those above you in the organization to lighten their load by dumping some of it on you.

In reality, this is rarely the case. Many managers today view problem-solving and decision making as key skills that often separate the more talented employees from those who would rather wait for someone else to tell them what to do. If you have the right skills and use them effectively, you can set yourself apart as a person who is ready and able to make important contributions to your job and your company. The message is, "I am accountable, involved, and committed to making things work around here." If you are not sure whether you have the right skills yet or if you feel you need to practice different approaches before you jump into real-world situations, this chapter can help you build confidence and competence.

We will examine a process for solving problems and describe a few techniques that will allow you to take charge of your job and fix your own problems. We will look at ways you can apply "cause-and-effect analysis" techniques to both routine and complex situations, ways you can resolve problems and not just point a finger or find someone else to blame. We will emphasize evaluating solutions using the same quality, time, and cost criteria introduced in Chapter One:

- How quickly can you determine causes and correct the problem?
- How quickly can you make and implement the solution?
- How good is the solution or decision? Is it rational, logical, and acceptable to others?
- How much will it cost?

In this chapter, we will focus on a rational, systematic approach to problem-solving and decision making but will leave the door open for more creative techniques that are important components of the next chapter's emphasis on innovation and flexibility.

Step One: Recognize and Admit That There Is a Problem

A problem is basically an undesirable situation in which things are different from the way you would like them to be or different from the way they used to be. Problem-solving is an attempt to explain something that has happened in the past so that you can take appropriate actions to shape the future the way you want it to be. There are four typical ways people tend to deal with problems:

1. They take an *inactive* approach, ignore the situation, and hope it will simply go away with little or no personal involvement.
2. They take a *reactive* approach, determine what has gone wrong, analyze the cause of the problem, and take steps to remedy the situation as quickly and as effectively as possible.
3. They take an *overreactive* approach, panic, catastrophize, and reach for quick band-aid solutions that often make the situation worse.
4. They use a *proactive* approach to anticipate problems, prevent them from happening, or minimize their impact when they cannot be avoided.

Obviously, the first approach is problem avoidance and not problem solving. Although there will be occasions when it will be best for you to wait before acting, turning your back on a problem will never solve it.

The second approach is much more common, and you may find yourself reacting to problem situations on a regular basis.

The third approach, overreacting, usually happens when there is a crisis and decisions need to be made quickly, leaving little time for logical planning. It is not a problem-solving technique and often further complicates the situation.

The fourth approach, being proactive, requires planning. This takes time and energy. Many people stay so busy reacting to real problems (firefighting) they do not have time to prepare for the next crisis (fire-prevention).

Take a few minutes to complete the problem definition worksheet in Figure 6-1 to define a problem that you are currently dealing with or have recently dealt with on your job. At this time, do not try to identify causes, effects, or solutions. Focus, instead, on simply stating a problem you have recognized as important.

- What has gone wrong?
- How serious is the problem?
- How frequently does it occur?
- Where and when did the problem begin?
- What is different from the past when things were moving toward a desired outcome or the situation was more desirable than it is now?

Step Two: Develop a Clear and Concise Problem Statement

Before analyzing the causes and effects of this problem, state it clearly in language that will be helpful to you and to anyone else you may decide to involve in your problem-solving efforts. You may discover later that your original understanding of the problem needs some modification, but your initial problem statement can help you make some strategic decisions about how to proceed. Use the problem statement form in Figure 6-2 to capture as precisely as you can the real problem. Here are a few sample problem statements that focus exclusively on the facts:

- We have a significant backlog of requisitions, invoices, and vendor inquiries. At last count, yesterday afternoon, there were more than 100 items that needed immediate attention. This situation has never occurred before.

Figure 6-1. Problem definition.

What has gone wrong?

```
┌─────────────────────────────────────────────────────┐
│                                                       │
│                                                       │
│                                                       │
│                                                       │
└─────────────────────────────────────────────────────┘
```

How serious is the problem?

```
┌─────────────────────────────────────────────────────┐
│                                                       │
│                                                       │
│                                                       │
│                                                       │
└─────────────────────────────────────────────────────┘
```

How frequently does it occur?

```
┌─────────────────────────────────────────────────────┐
│                                                       │
│                                                       │
│                                                       │
│                                                       │
└─────────────────────────────────────────────────────┘
```

Where and when did the problem begin?

```
┌─────────────────────────────────────────────────────┐
│                                                       │
│                                                       │
│                                                       │
│                                                       │
└─────────────────────────────────────────────────────┘
```

What's different from before when things were moving toward a desired outcome or the situation was more desirable than it is now?

```
┌─────────────────────────────────────────────────────┐
│                                                       │
│                                                       │
│                                                       │
│                                                       │
└─────────────────────────────────────────────────────┘
```

Figure 6-2. Problem statement form.

The real problem I am concerned about is:

The problem statement records several important details—the problem is a new one, it is significant, and it may involve two different solutions—how to fix the current problem and how to prevent it from happening again. Although the person probably has some ideas about possible causes of the problem (like recent downsizing activities), or potential negative effects of the problem (like loss of customers and lower employee morale), there is no attempt made at this time to go beyond a clear statement of the problem.

■ I am spending two extra hours each week writing monthly status reports about our production activities, our safety performance, and our overtime schedules.

Again, the initial statement does not mention the impact or effect the problem is having. For example, the person making the statement does not say "these administrative tasks are making it more and more difficult for me to complete my more important technical tasks." The problem statement is a brief, specific summary of the undesirable situation.

■ For the third time this month, the applications I need from the processing department arrived too late for me to meet my deadline. Some of the applications were incorrect or incomplete and had to be returned.

The focus is on the details of the problem as a starting point to examine causes and arrive at satisfactory solutions.

Step Three: Determine the Approach You Want to Take to Resolve the Problem

There are several facts you need to examine at this point in the process. All of them can help you determine the best way to move forward. Use Figure 6-3 to record your answers to the following questions:

Figure 6-3. An assessment of your approach.

Level of Importance

Degree of Impact on You

Degree of Impact on Others

Actual Negative Effects

Your Level of Involvement

Your Role

Benefits to You

- How important is this problem to you and your performance?

- What impact is this problem having on your ability to do your job efficiently and effectively?

- What impact is this problem having on your work group, your department, your company?

- What are some negative effects you can identify resulting from this problem? Consider and list as many as you can document or prove. For example, your list might include time lost having to redo mistakes, unnecessary overtime, lost customers, increased number of complaints, morale problems, reduced quantity or quality of work, damaged working relationships with others, or unnecessary expenses. Focus here on the *actual* negative effects.

- What are some *potential* negative effects you anticipate happening as a result of this problem? Your list might include some of the same items you uncovered when you answered the previous questions. For example, you may know that you have already lost a few customers and that you will continue to do so if the problem is not resolved. You may also have a hunch that your company is running the risk of losing a few talented employees if this problem is not corrected. It has not happened yet, but you have a feeling it might.

- How involved do you need to be in resolving this problem? How much ownership and accountability do you need to have in fixing this situation? This is a key point in your decision-making process about how you want to address this problem. Do you have the time right now to attack this issue? Is it important enough to make the problem a priority and find the time to resolve it? Are the benefits associated with resolving the problem greater than the costs of doing something about it now, or should you let it go for a while? Will the quality or quantity of your current work be adversely affected if you devote time and energy to this issue?

- What role should you play in resolving this problem? If the problem is directly related to your own job and is affecting your job performance, you need to empower yourself and take a leadership role in fixing the problem. You may need to bring in others to help you understand and correct the situation, but you are in charge of what needs to be done. If you do not feel you have adequate authority to act independently on this problem, you need to get the support you need from your manager. Remember, you are not asking for a solution. You are asking for the authority to proceed with a process you know you can handle with approval from above. If the problem is indirectly related to your own performance or if it is too complex for you to attempt to resolve on your own, you may still benefit from taking a leadership role in which you bring others together to develop a solution. Once you have initiated the process, you may decide that you need to shift to a more secondary role, maybe as a member of a team that you helped organize or as a valued contributor at regular meetings designed to explore and resolve similar problems.

■ What benefits will you receive from resolving this problem? Before you move on to the next step in the process, list two or three of the major benefits you will receive by attacking this problem now. These motivations can help you charge up your batteries as you get ready to launch what may be a difficult, frustrating, and time-consuming activity.

Once you have determined the approach you intend to take and the benefits you will realize when you do, shift your focus to the data collection process that will get you the results you need.

1. Start by identifying the kind of information you will need to define the problem. If the information is readily available, part of your routine activities, you only need to record specific examples or document what you have experienced or observed. This activity helps you analyze patterns or trends. For example, if another department has been late getting you information you need to do your job, a list of dates, times, and impact on you is probably enough to get started.

You may decide, for example, that you need to talk to other people in person, by telephone, or by e-mail. You may decide that a survey questionnaire can give you quick and anonymous feedback from key individuals. You may decide that bringing a small focus group together can help you brainstorm the issue and possible causes. In all cases, it is important for you to state why you need the information you are collecting and how you plan to use it. At this point, confidentiality is critical, and your credibility is at stake. Remember, this is not a witch-hunt or an attempt to point your finger at others. Your sole interest is resolving a problem so that things can get back on track for you and your coworkers.

2. Record and summarize the data in a format that will make it easy for you to share with others. Consider visuals—charts, graphs, checklists—and short reports. Keep the data as concise, current, and precise as possible.

3. Analyze the data you have collected for patterns or trends. Avoid subjective interpretation of what the information means. Postpone judg-

ment until you have the complete picture. Try using one of the following techniques to help you understand the real cause of the problem:

- Review the history of the problem by listing key dates associated with it. When did it start? Has it ever gotten better? Has it ever gotten worse? Has it ever gone away completely? When did it re-occur?
- After you have listed specific occasions, you may be able to see trends. You may also be able to get a better understanding of causes and possible solutions. For example, the problem chronology chart in Figure 6-4 can help you make educated guesses about why the

Figure 6-4. Chronological analysis chart and problem timeline.

Chronological Analysis Chart

Symptom/ Cause	When did it start?	What happened then?	Why?
A.			
B.			
C.			

Problem Timeline

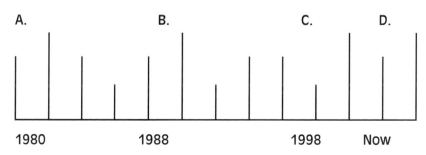

problem reoccurred in 1998 after a ten-year hiatus and why it surfaced again in such a short time.

■ After you have stated the problem, ask yourself a series of open-ended questions: Why did this happen? When did it start? What role did I play in creating the problem? What should I do to resolve it? What can I do to prevent it from happening again? Write down as many questions as you can, answer them honestly, and then put your list aside for a few hours. When you pick it up again, start by seeing if there are any additional questions you want to add or any new answers or insights. If you think it will help, repeat the process one more time. Then review the chart in Figure 6-5 for causes and possible solutions.

Once you have collected and analyzed data about the causes of the problem, you are in a much better position to decide how you want to resolve it. Every problem-solving activity ultimately leads to a decision-making process. You move from explaining something that has happened in the past—the problem—to determining what you want to happen in the future—your solution. There are a variety of tools and techniques available to help you analyze your options and make the best choice. Try using the following action steps:

Start with a clear statement. What do you want to happen in the near future? What do you want to happen on an ongoing basis? What do you want to prevent happening from now on? For example, if you wanted to resolve the word processing backlog (described in Figure 6-5), your initial decision statement might include goals like "reduce the backlog by 10 percent each week until it has been cleared up" or "make sure there are no preferred customers in the current work backlog."

Define the ideal solution as specifically as you can. The challenge here is to list and prioritize the criteria you will use to make the best decision. What factors do you need or want to consider as you try to resolve this problem? Some common criteria include:

■ *Quantity of work.* Measured by factual information like productivity levels, number of reports completed, and other calculations of output, outcomes, and results.

■ *Quality of work.* Measured in terms of rejects, repeat work, customer complaints, communication breakdowns, missed deadlines, and other indicators of poor service or response time. Positive measurements—customer compliments and industry awards—can also be used.

Figure 6-5. Repetitive why analysis chart.

The problem: There is a backlog of work, over twenty-five different reports, in the word processing unit.

Why did this occur? It was caused by . . .

An attempt to centralize word processing in one area under one supervisor.

Why did this occur? It was caused by . . .

Recent company downsizing efforts to streamline decision-making activities and improve quality control.

Why did this occur? It was caused by . . .

A corporate-wide push to reduce costs by identifying key customers and paying careful attention to their needs.

Why did this occur? It was caused by . . .

An understanding that certain nonpreferred customers could not receive the same type of attention they did in the past. What might have been important activities last year would need to be reevaluated and reprioritized so that pre-ferred customers got satisfactory attention. Backlogs would occur and would need to be addressed on an item-by-item basis.

Root Cause

- *Cost criteria.* Any of the financial indicators such as budget and expenses that put limits on spending or define acceptable gains to be achieved. To allow room for flexibility, cost criteria are often stated in ranges of "no more than" or "no less than."
- *Time criteria.* Based on schedules, deadlines, and any other com-

mitments about when a particular task or activity needs to be completed or a target date connected to some other event (before our new Main Street store opens).

- *Risk and safety criteria.* Any policies or procedures established to protect you, other employees, and your company.
- *The impact your decision will have on others* is another factor that may not have clear measurement criteria until you develop them. In this area, you will want to consider any potential negative impact your decision might have: Will you ruffle anyone's feathers? Will you put yourself or your manager in an awkward position? Will others be jealous or resentful of the initiative you have taken? Will your solution create additional work for someone else? The answers to these questions might affect your final decision.

Determine which criteria are most significant. For example, is it more important for you to stay within budget than to meet a specific deadline? Would it be better for your company if you produce a dozen exceptional products instead of the twenty "cut-corner" samples your customer has requested? Will the safety training required to operate this new piece of equipment justify the investment of time, energy, and money?

The challenge is to decide which factors are the most important as you move forward in the process. One technique that can help you sort out the criteria is to ask yourself "What *must* happen?—Absolutely no room for error or flexibility!" Then ask, "What would be a nice-to-have benefit?"—something that should add another positive element to your decision.

Once you have prioritized and defined your criteria, you can list them on a form like the criteria matrix in Figure 6-6. It is important to be as specific as possible about the criteria you have chosen. In the example shown, notice how each criterion is spelled out as clearly as possible:

- *Cost.* Expenses cannot exceed $38,000 over the next nine months.
- *Time.* Project must be completed no later than April 15, 2001.
- *Risk.* Every effort must be made to satisfy the service needs of 95 percent of our customer base. The potential loss of five preferred customers will be considered an unacceptable risk.
- *Quality.* The output of the process must meet industry standards and the product specifications provided by at least twenty preferred customers over the past ten years.

Figure 6-6. Sample criteria matrix.

Rating Scale: Does the solution meet the criterion?—Yes/No/Unsure   How well does the solution meet the criterion?—1 to 5   Are there more positives, negatives, or unknowns with this solution?—+/−/?

Possible Solution	Time	Cost	Risk	Quality	Rating
	Project must be completed no later than April 15, 2001.	Expenses can not exceed $38,000 over the next nine months.	The potential loss of five preferred customers will be considered an unacceptable risk.	The output of the process must meet industry standards.	

CASE STUDY

Hunter H. has been assigned responsibility for streamlining processes and procedures in his company's customer service department. There have been some significant problems with backlogs,
customer complaints, and missed deadlines. Hunter's manager
has asked him to determine the causes of these problems and to
recommend some ways to resolve them.

Your Analysis

Before reviewing Hunter's approach to this problem, take a few
minutes to write down some of your ideas about this situation.
What would you do and why?

_____

_____

_____

The Employee's Actions

After Hunter collected enough data to define the problem and
identify several possible causes, he realized that the biggest
problem in the department was the way work was being distributed. He and the other customer service representatives were
not giving enough time and attention to their better customers.
The process was haphazard, based more on alphabetical than priority order. The backlog problem had a similar root cause—things
got done in the order they were received rather than by order of
importance. Using this information, Hunter met with his manager and suggested that they consider either changing the structure of the department or the way it would operate in the future.
Hunter assured his manager that he had several ideas to improve
operations but that he needed clarification about some of the
criteria they would use to analyze their options. Together, they
developed a criteria matrix (Figure 6-6), which Hunter then used
to present four possible solutions (Figure 6-7).

❖   ❖   ❖   ❖   ❖

A criteria chart becomes a useful tool when you list as many possible
solutions as you can on the left of the chart and then plot known facts in
each appropriate box.

Figure 6-7. Filled-out criteria matrix.

Rating Scale: Does the solution meet the criterion?—Yes/No/Unsure   How well does the solution meet the criterion?—1 to 5   Are there more positives, negatives, or unknowns with this solution?—+/−/?

Possible Solution	Time *Project must be completed no later than April 15, 2001.*	Cost *Expenses can not exceed $38,000 over the next nine months.*	Risk *The potential loss of five preferred customers will be considered an unacceptable risk.*	Quality *The output of the process must meet industry standards.*	Rating
A. Combine customer service and sales functions and cross-train all department employees.	YES (Can be done with some inconvenience)	YES	NO (Significant potential of losing customers during reorganization)	NO (Defining common standards would be time-consuming)	Low Positive
B. Assign ten preferred customers to each account representative so they can establish and maintain effective long-term relationships with these customers.	YES (Can be implemented quickly after key accounts have been identified)	YES (Minimal)	YES (Minimal risk if right account representatives are selected)	YES (Should improve quality of service)	High Positive
C. Hire twelve additional account reps over the next six months to provide coverage for expected growth of customer base.	UNSURE (Depends on available talent)	NO (Salaries and benefits)	YES (Relatively safe if people are trained well)	UNSURE (Depends on caliber of people hired)	Negative (too many variables)
D. Do nothing now and see what develops by the end of the year.	YES (No impact)	YES (No cost)	NO (Increase potential for lost customers)	NO (Current quality problems will only get worse)	Negative

After listing what options or choices are potentially workable, use the criteria you have selected to evaluate each option. Eliminate any alternatives that do not meet your criteria, then select the best one. Review the example (Figure 6-7) that shows how Hunter's company used the criteria matrix to reorganize its customer service department.

Once you have identified the best alternatives, do a cost/benefit analysis to make certain you have considered all of the benefits (the positive outcomes) and all of the costs (the negative implications) of this particular option. A cost/benefit analysis form (Figure 6-8) is a useful tool to give you a quick graphic look at the action you are considering. State the action

Figure 6-8. Cost/benefit analysis.

Action You Are Considering: _____

	Benefits/Positives (+'s)	*Costs/Negatives* (−'s)
If You Take This Action	A.	B.
If You Don't Take This Action	C.	D.

A + D > B + C . . . Do it!

A + D < B + C . . . Don't do it

A + D = B + C . . . Get more information

at the top of the form, then fill in the appropriate boxes with as many pros and cons as you can think of.

This type of graphic can provide a quick picture, a good reality check of the pros and cons of your decision.

Finally, develop a contingency plan to make sure you are prepared to deal with anything that could possibly go wrong. If you can anticipate any negative consequences from the action you plan to take, decide what you can do now to prevent potential problems. How can you minimize their impact if you cannot stop the problems from happening? Start by listing as many things you can think of that could possibly go wrong with your plan.

Use statements that force you to consider "what would happen if . . .":

- Your current priorities are juggled and new projects are added to your already "full plate" of activities?
- Equipment problems occur?
- Budget cuts are announced?
- One of your key coworkers resigns?
- Your manager is promoted and replaced by someone from another department?
- Your vendors increase their charges by more than the 15 percent you expected?
- The winter months are more severe than they have been recently and your delivery schedules are affected?

Review your list and do a quick risk analysis by asking yourself, "How likely is it that this contingency will occur?" and "How serious will it be if it does?" If you have high scores for both of these questions, you may have identified a risky situation that will require serious attention.

If your contingency analysis does not bring to the surface any potentially high-risk situations, move comfortably on to the final step in the process. Implement your decision. Keep track of how you have decided to solve the problem so that you can document your success, fine-tune where modifications are necessary, and use data from this problem-solving activity to help you with future problems.

If you have never been challenged before to solve your own work problems, this process might seem intimidating the first time you try it. There are a number of related action steps and a variety of techniques that you can use to go from your initial problem statement to a satisfactory resolution. What may seem, at first, like a time-consuming process gets easier every time you use it. The tools provided here also give you a set of visual support documents to help you lead someone else through your thought process. If that person is your manager, another decision maker, or a coworker who will be affected by your decision, you will have charts and tables to show how you completed key parts of the process. Each of these charts can be developed, saved, and presented to defend, support, or justify your decision. You may also want to use the abbreviated problem solving summary sheet in Figure 6-9 to highlight your key decision points.

Figure 6-9. Problem-solving summary sheet.

Action Steps: Analyze the Situation

- Describe what was happening before.
- Describe what is happening now.
- Describe what must happen soon (near future).
- Describe what must happen later (down the line).
- Describe what caused this problem to occur.
- Describe the effect this problem is having on you or others.

- Describe the benefits of solving the problem.
- Describe the consequences of **not** solving the problem.
- Decide whether the problem is significant or urgent enough to address at this time.

Before	Now	Soon	Later
Cause	Effect	Benefit	
		Consequence	

Action Steps: Solve the Problem

- Define the outcome you want or need in specific terms using any or all of the four major performance criteria: quantity, quality, time, and cost.
- List one alternative and assess its potential value or possible negative effects.
- Select the best solution and be able to describe your decision-making process to others who need or want to know.

Desired Outcome				
Alternative	**Quantity**	**Quality**	**Time**	**Cost**

Analyze facts and data carefully before attempting to resolve a problem. Make high-quality and timely decisions when problems arise. Be sure your decisions and solutions are consistent with your company's core values and key objectives. Use a variety of problem-solving techniques depending on the situation and the people involved. Get information and help from others in making important decisions. Let others who should be informed know about your decisions. Try new ways of resolving problems and be willing to take risks when you are investigating different approaches. Although a data-based, logical process may be most appropriate most of the time, you should be prepared to use different techniques whenever you have room for innovation and flexibility. Taking a more creative approach to problem-solving is the subject of our next chapter.

7

Be Creative and Flexible: Look for Innovative Solutions and New Approaches

Don't fear failure so much that you refuse to try new things. The saddest summary of a life contains three descriptions: could have, might have, and should have.

> —Louis E. Boone, American educator and business writer

The creative process is any thinking which solves a problem in an original and useful way

> —Herbert Fox, scholar

Scientists have known for a long time that the brain has two distinct hemispheres. The left controls movements on the body's right side; the right controls movements on the left. Additional research has demonstrated that the two hemispheres are specialized in more fundamental ways. It has been proven that the left side of the brain controls our logical thinking processes. It is linear, and it processes information sequentially, one bit after another in an ordered way. It is the area of the brain that stores code words for objects and things. Language is the most critical linear function of the left side of the brain.

The words most often associated with the left side of the brain include *analytical, intellectual, verbal, explicit, rational,* and *logical*. It is the part of the brain you use to debate issues, to clarify your position in an argument, to weigh options and select the best one, and to help you make informed decisions. It is the side of the brain you used for most of the problem-solving and decision-making activities in the previous chapter.

The right side of the brain controls creative thinking processes. It processes information simultaneously. It is the area of the brain that is holistic, "big picture," spontaneous, and innovative. The most critical right brain function is the comprehension of visual images. The words most often associated with the right brain include *experiential, implicit, relational, exploratory,* and *imaginative.* It is in the right side of the brain where new discoveries are born, where you have those "Eureka!" moments and "Aha!" experiences. You will have a chance to try using the right side of your brain for the creative problem-solving and decision-making activities described in this chapter.

There are times when you will use only one side of your brain to solve a problem or make a decision. There are times when the best approach will require shifting from one side of the brain to the other, applying a combination of processes. There are also times when the situation or problem itself will limit your choices. Let's consider how these factors come into play.

First, you probably have a preferred decision-making style based on past experiences. You tend to gravitate toward either a rational or creative approach depending on your current comfort level. As mentioned in the previous chapter, many of us have been taught to take a logical approach to problems. Therefore, we have more experience with left-brain, analytical thinking, and our comfort level is higher when using skills and techniques associated with linear processes. Many people who say they are not creative often describe themselves as being more comfortable with a rational approach. It does not mean, however, that they cannot or will not be creative, but it does mean that a creative approach would not be their first or favorite choice.

Another potential barrier to creative thinking has to do with the length of time you have worked in a particular job. The longer you have performed your current job function, the easier it is for you to become blind to your own mistakes. If you have ever tried to proofread one of your own reports, you know how easy it is to overlook mistakes and pass over even the most obvious grammatical errors. Computer spellcheck software can help with spelling problems, but unless you slow down your editing activities to a word-by-word pace, some embarrassing mistakes can turn up in the wrong hands. In such cases, you have become too close to your own work, blind to errors that are all too obvious to someone looking at your writing with a fresh pair of eyes. Important problems can occur before you notice even the earliest warning signals, the smallest indication that something is going wrong.

The only way to protect yourself from these oversights is to step back from your work occasionally and try to view it from a different, more objective perspective. Open your eyes to what is really happening by reviewing processes, procedures, and activities that are taking up most of your time, and then decide if they are contributing to your priority objectives. Being on the alert for bottlenecks, breakdowns, and potential problem areas will protect you from narrow vision and from seeing only what you expect to see or want to see. This approach is similar to defensive driving. You keep the car moving forward toward your ultimate destination—your priority goal and objective—while paying careful attention to what is going on around you. Your peripheral vision lets you see potential dangers, anticipate problems, and prepare for unexpected roadblocks. This attention to your surrounding environment may also simply confirm that everything around you is fine for now. There is a smooth, safe, and uneventful journey ahead. No need to create problems if there are none, but also no need to stop looking again sometime in the near future. Regular vigilance is the best safeguard against being lulled into overlooking problems that may be obvious to everyone else.

Of course, there are hundreds of other ways that good ideas can be shot down before they are given a chance to fly. In fact, these killer phrases have become fairly routine:

- It will never work, never succeed, never get us the results we want.
- It's too risky, too expensive, too revolutionary, too late.
- It looks good on paper, but. . . .
- Our customers (suppliers, vendors, managers, coworkers) will never go for this idea.
- We already have a lot going on, too much work to be distracted by something new, policies and procedures in place to deal with this type of problem.
- Why should we complicate our lives now?
- Let's sit on it for a while and see what happens.
- Let's not rush into something that has been a problem for twenty-five years and will be here when we all retire.
- Are you crazy?
- Who are you trying to impress?

In his 1980 AMA Management Briefing, "Idea Management," Charles H. Clark describes Rule 816, one of those humorous "laws" that had appeared in American companies. It read:

Rule 816 is now in effect until further notice. When confronted with a new idea, vote against it because:

- It is probably not a good idea; new ideas seldom are.
- Even if it is a good idea, the chances are it will never be tested.
- Even if it is a good idea, and even though it is tested, chances are that it won't work the first time.
- Even if it is a good idea, and even though it is tested, and even if it succeeds, there'll be plenty of time for thinking up alibis.

Therefore: When confronted with a new idea, the rational action is to take a positive and forward-looking stand against it.

Author Edward de Bono describes this approach as looking for the "no" in creative thinking rather than trying to find the "po"—the potential, the possibilities, the power of new ideas.

Creative people have developed a variety of techniques that can help you in your efforts:

- Write down your ideas in a notebook, journal, or pocket calendar. Do not trust your busy memory to recall things that get bumped aside in your brain almost as quickly as you try to store them away. Then make it a point to review your notes regularly. You may be amazed to learn how fertile your mind really is, and you may find some valuable seeds that are worth nurturing and developing.

- Limit your time—ten or fifteen minutes usually works—so that you force yourself to be concise. Don't worry about grammar, spelling, or complete sentences. A list of bullets is usually best. Don't try to connect your ideas. For now, you are racing against your own self-imposed time limits. Quantity of information is more important than quality at this point. If something pops into your head that does not make sense, write it down and keep going. You will be able to make connections later. When your time is up, look at your list and add any explanatory notes you want.

- Suspend judgment about new ideas, then focus initially on as many positives as you can—how this idea can help you solve a problem, how your manager and others will appreciate your efforts, how you can work this idea into your already busy schedule. Instead of being overly critical and reverting to any of those killer phrases, be optimistic about the possibilities of this new idea. Something about it was important enough for you to write it down. For now, take care of what you have planted, and do not be tempted to kill the idea or abandon it prematurely.

- Use free association, the process of connecting related ideas with each other in a somewhat random way. For example, the word *budget* might lead you to a list of associated words like *money, salary, bonus, performance review, promotion,* and *job satisfaction.*

- Focus on one particular opportunity, issue, or concern, and record as much information as you can about what you need or want to do. Television correspondent Bill Moyers once described this type of concentration as a cornerstone of the creative process: "Creativity requires that we stop paying general attention to everything in order to pay particular attention to something." Once you have funneled your thinking to a specific topic, let your brain take over for a while.

- Be open to your experiences. Relax and go with the flow for a while. Try not to shoot down your own good ideas too quickly.

- Clear the slate and start from scratch whenever you can. Put aside any preconceived notions that automatically interfere with new approaches. Be flexible, not rigid, in the way you look at things.

- Make a commitment to see things differently and to allow yourself enough time to play around with new ideas. Be persistent and patient. If creative thinking is a new activity for you, give yourself some time to experiment with the process.

- If you want to expand or accelerate this creative process or if you need a reality check to evaluate your ideas, invite others to join in your efforts. Pick people who are creative and willing to share in your thought process rather then superimposing their own.

There are two popular techniques you can use to bring others into your creative problem-solving activities. The first is called "brainstorming."

Alex Osborn developed brainstorming as a process for addressing advertising and marketing problems. He encouraged participants to postpone any critical judgment during the process and realize the potential of an approach designed to build and not kill creativity. He defined brainstorming as "a way to collect a number of ideas verbally from a group in a very short period of time and to vote on the most viable ones." The steps he developed include:

1. Identify the topic you want to brainstorm and emphasize action by asking a specific "how" question: How can we improve productivity?

How can we reduce expenses? How should we respond to our customers' concerns?

2. Each member of the brainstorming team for ideas in rotation. Participants may offer only *one* idea each time it is their turn. Participants who do not have an idea when it is their turn say "Pass." Ideas are listed on a flipchart or board so that everyone can see them. This continues until all ideas have been exhausted.

3. No ideas suggested should be evaluated. In fact, there should be no comments made at all at this time about someone else's ideas. The purpose for now is to generate as many ideas as possible.

4. After all ideas have been listed, review each idea to make sure the group understands what has been presented (still no evaluation or judgment, only clarification).

5. After all the ideas have been clarified, have participants prioritize them by polling or voting. People may vote for as many ideas as they want. You should record only supporting votes, so encourage participants to vote for any idea they feel has value.

6. After you have circled those ideas that received the most votes, have participants vote again to rank the ideas in priority order.

7. You now have identified the most viable ideas or suggestions. You also have a list of other options you will want to save for future consideration.

Another popular technique to involve others in your creative problem-solving efforts is called "Crawford Slip Writing." University of California Professor C. C. Crawford developed this process and defined it as "a way to collect a number of anonymous ideas from a group in a very short period of time." The steps he suggested include:

1. Give members a pad of 3x5 papers or a stack of index cards.
2. Present a specific problem or opportunity statement in "how do we" question format.
3. Encourage each team member to hold back judgments, fight "killer phrases," and write down as many answers to the question as possible in a specified period of time.
4. Ask members to put each answer on a separate slip of paper or index card.
5. Collect and sort the responses, then evaluate the ideas through discussion and more slip writing. In a short time, you will have collected a number of anonymous ideas. Some can be applied immediately. Others can be saved for future use.

The slip writing technique can also be used:

- To identify potential problems or opportunities. (How do we prevent? How do we minimize the impact of? How do we capitalize on this trend?)
- To resolve complex problems that have multiple symptoms, causes, or solutions.
- To evaluate a possible decision and decide the best ways to modify or implement it.

Of course, there are occasions when you will be challenged to use your least favorite approach. If you need to build a case to defend your decision, a logical, data-based process may be your only option. That will be a stretch for you if you are, by nature, a creative person. If the situation requires a solution that goes beyond traditional, tried-and-true options, you will need to use a creative process, even if that would not be your preferred choice. Finally, there will be times when you need to shift from one side of the brain to the other, combining both logical and creative thinking that moves you from relevant information to innovative solutions. If you are not sure of your preferred decision-making style, take a few minutes to answer the following self-assessment questions.

Think about the way you typically make decisions or solve problems, and check off one item in each set of questions that *best* describes your usual style of behavior.

1. When faced with an important organizational issue or decision I usually prefer:

- ☐ To come to conclusions by myself after carefully reviewing and thinking about information presented.
- ☐ To "think aloud" or brainstorm with my associates as a way of gathering additional ideas, options, or possibilities.

2. I consider myself:

- ☐ A very practical and pragmatic person. I rely on facts, firsthand experience, proven realities, common sense, and sound standards in making decisions.
- ☐ An intuitive person. I depend on new insights, creative inspirations, "gut feelings," and big-picture associations in making decisions.

3. I usually make decisions or solve problems:

❏ In an impartial, logical way based on available data. I value fairness, competency, objectivity, and evenhandedness in dealing with others. I can usually determine and implement the smart, sensible, logical solution.

❏ In a way that considers how solutions will affect people. I value helping others, compassion, and support. I place a high value on the personal implications of a decision, on harmony, and on including the needs and wishes of others in my decisions.

4. In my general work behavior:

❏ I have a high need for closure and being in control. I prefer leading a very planned and scheduled life. I am often impatient with indecision, delays, inefficiency, and any activity that tends to waste my time. I'd rather make the wrong decision quickly and have to modify it than to make no decision at all.

❏ I am flexible and adaptable. I like to keep things open-ended, loose, and informal. I do not emphasize protocol, control, or strict procedures. I believe people work best in an environment where there is some freedom, a sense of togetherness and equality, a feeling of open communication, and a dynamic flow of new ideas across all levels of the organization.

Think about a recent situation in which your usual style of behavior helped you make a good decision or solve a problem. What factors made the outcome successful?

Now think about a recent situation in which the outcome was not as successful as you anticipated. What factors produced less than desirable results?

Now that you have identified whether you prefer a rational, creative, or balanced approach, you can decide whether you need to develop skills in any particular area. You can also decide how a specific approach will help you with different problems, especially when there are organizational or operational restrictions. There are several questions you should ask yourself about the situation before you proceed:

▪ How much freedom do you have with this issue? Have you been empowered to come up with something new and different, or is this a case of a quick "whatever works" solution?

■ How much time can you dedicate to solving this problem or making this decision? The logical, rational approach can take more time because you are gathering information and documenting the process as you go along. The creative approach may actually be faster, and the results are often described as flashes of inspiration, break-through moments, and leaps of faith.

■ Do you need or want to involve others in the decision-making process? What strengths will they bring to your collaborative efforts? What is their preferred style of dealing with problems?

■ How complex is the problem? How urgent? How important? Is there room for experimentation? Can you play around with possibilities, test options, and do some trial runs with creative alternatives?

■ How much accountability do you have in this situation? Do you own both the problem and the solution? Will you get credit for a good idea? Are you willing to take or share the blame if your idea does not work? Do you have your manager's support and cooperation from everyone else who will be affected by your decision?

Once you have determined your preferred style and examined the situation carefully, you will be able to use either the rational decision-making skills described in the previous chapter or the creative techniques described in this chapter. With practice you should be able to shift between right and left brain activities and combine approaches if the situation requires a balanced process.

Let's focus now on creative problem-solving, the approach you will want to take when you have the urge to innovate, to examine new possibilities, to come up with something that no one has ever tried. Creativity involves trying a new approach, one that goes beyond traditional methods, one that breaks free of a "not invented here" mentality.

The nineteenth-century French mathematician Henri Poincaré was among the first to propose what are still regarded as the basic steps in creative problem-solving.

1. The first stage is *preparation.* You immerse yourself in the problem and search out any relevant information. You collect a broad range of data so that any unusual details begin to emerge. This is active work based on a confident belief that you will be able to see connections and visualize new possibilities. It involves a leap of faith that this random process of collecting information (panning for gold) will lead to some amazing discoveries (that one priceless nugget).

2. The second stage is *incubation*. Once you have framed the problem and gathered only the most pertinent information, you should let the problem simmer for awhile. This is passive work, a time to sleep on the problem, a time to trust your intuition and your gut feelings. Creative people often describe a variety of activities they associate with this stage of the process—daydreaming, meditation, quiet walks, driving to work, and other things they do by themselves once they have cleared their minds of distractions.

3. The third stage is *illumination*. Somehow a solution comes to you, a new idea springs forward, a novel approach takes shape mysteriously and develops into a workable alternative. Most creative people cannot explain how this happens, and, in fact, they do not even try to understand it. What they know is that it usually works.

4. The fourth stage is *translation*. The idea must be applied and tested. Other people must find the idea useful and take it seriously. An innovative solution is different from one that has been done before. People need to feel confident that it will work. Therefore, creative acts are both unique and useful. They must work. To be creative the idea must make sense. It must be meaningful and helpful. How a creative idea is received is very important.

Scientists who study creative problem-solving practices often describe four building blocks of creativity:

1. *Imagination*. The willingness to take risks, the courage to try something new, the determination to relinquish control of your thinking mind and trust your unconscious to provide answers.

2. *Knowledge*. The ability to draw information from your past experiences and to apply your expertise to the current situation. How you use information, how you make sense of it, therefore, is often as important as the information itself.

3. *Curiosity*. The kind of inquisitiveness that makes you want to go below the tip of the iceberg and explore what is going on beneath the surface. It means being interested in discovering things that are not immediately apparent, searching for hidden patterns, connecting ideas that do not usually belong together, working on both comparisons and contrasts so you can see how some things are the same and some are different. It often means enjoying the journey more than arriving at your destination.

4. *Persistence*. The willingness to stick with a problem and not give in to personal disappointment, cynicism, negative thinking, or frustration. It also means the ability to deal with others who may be pressuring you

to find the one best solution as quickly as you can so you can move on to other activities. It means having the patience to stop imagining all the reasons why your idea will never work and start listing ways you can make it a success. In 1899, Charles H. Duell, commissioner of the U.S. Office of Patents, said in a report to President McKinley, "Everything that can be invented has been invented." He had apparently given up his belief in American ingenuity.

Even in today's fast-paced workplace, many companies are paying close attention to the way people gather, interpret, and apply information. This information is the material from which new ideas are formed. It's like playing with a ball of clay that you begin working around in your hands. As your fingers start forming a fish, your mind begins telling you the clay object is more like a bird. Then you gradually see a horse emerging, and you realize that what you actually created is something resembling a wolf sitting on the table in front of you.

It's the same with new ideas. You play around with the data at hand, and by pulling and poking at the available information, Aha! experiences start to occur. New patterns and shapes emerge. What seemed at first like the best options become less viable alternatives. The more you are willing to suspend judgment, the more likely you are to visualize other possibilities. By allowing your creative mind the opportunity to wander and play with the intellectual clay you have to work with, you will be amazed at the number of new ideas that you can generate in a very short time.

Companies are now realizing that encouraging people to look for one best answer can seriously limit their ability to find multiple options and new opportunities. These companies have come to appreciate the importance of supporting a more creative approach so that value is placed on the process of doing the work and not just on the results or final product. Instead of fostering a "my way or the highway" mentality, companies are asking people at all levels to encourage and support each other so that everyone feels comfortable expressing new ideas without fear of criticism, ridicule, or punishment.

If you work in this type of creative environment, it will be easy for you to express openly and honestly even your most outrageous, off-the-wall ideas. If your company still puts some restrictions on innovation, the challenge for you will be to demonstrate the value of creative problem-solving in certain situations. Be selective and pick a few successes that show how creativity has helped you become more productive or helped your company become more profitable, efficient, or effective.

There are several significant barriers to creative thinking. For one, we do not need to be creative about most things in our lives. We develop and live routines that require little imaginative thinking. Once we are comfortable with the way we perform certain activities—tie our shoes, make coffee, balance our checkbook, mow the lawn, write reports—we rarely think about whether we need to change our approach or look for a better way.

We do the same thing with many of the processes in our lives. Once we have determined the best approach, we continue using it until something tells us to reevaluate what we are doing. We often take the same route to work every day, shop at the same supermarket, watch the same television shows, and take vacations in the same locations every year. We don't question or change our routine until something significant happens. Even then, we hold on to the old way of doing things for as long as we can. We use expressions such as "it's a tradition with us" or "we've always done it that way" to defend our reluctance to change old, familiar patterns. The comfort level we develop for most things in our lives makes creative thinking a difficult process for us.

Another significant barrier to creative thinking is the educational system we grew up in. More often than not, it encouraged us to look for one answer, the best solution, the most practical alternative, the only approach that makes sense. In many of our academic pursuits, we learned to pick true or false, yes or no, this or that, and then defend our choices in the most logical, rational way we could. Whenever we were tested, we preferred the objective, fill-in-the-blank type questions because they were clear and nondebatable—you either had the right answer or you were wrong. We enjoyed the freedom that the subjective essay questions gave us to display our widespread knowledge of almost any topic, but we often worried about how grading decisions would be made—it was our opinion versus our teacher's opinion. The challenge was to remember exactly what our teachers had said on the subject and then try to parrot or paraphrase their perspective as closely as we could. Our ability to play back their ideas often made the difference between a good grade and a passing one. Even when we were challenged to answer open-ended opinion questions, we usually knew that we were trying to remember what our teacher had told us to think about something that was completely unimportant to us.

These questions were definitely not exercises in creative thinking. They were more like memory tests to see how much we could recall from the information we had stored away for the occasion. Once the examination was over, and we had retrieved and used whatever we needed, we could hit the purge button, delete the unused data, and make space for the new information coming our way. The whole process, far from being creative, was a mechanical, logical activity with computer precision designed to get the right answer as quickly as possible. For most of us, this approach to thinking and finding solutions became our customary and comfortable way of making decisions.

As you saw in Chapter Six, there are many situations in which logical, rational, and data-based decision making is the only way you can resolve certain problems. You will need the weight of good information and a thoughtful process to convince others that you have developed a good solution. There are, however, occasions when you need to break away from these tried-and-true thought processes and try more creative approaches. When you do this, you need to convince yourself that what you are about to do has value and can produce some positive results. You need to open your mind to the potential of creative thinking and reduce your inherent skepticism that this approach may be a waste of time. You need to be optimistic that some good will come from a creative approach, and then jump into it with enthusiasm and determination.

Creative problem-solvers use a variety of the techniques listed below either as individual mental exercises or as part of group activities in which they enlist the help of others. Try them out and decide which ones would be most useful to you.

Technique 1: Decide to have some fun. Start by stating the problem, then ask yourself, "How would the Three Stooges deal with this one?" or "Would Laurel and Hardy take a different approach?" As you begin to think about their solutions, smile, jot down any idea that pops up, and let yourself appreciate that this problem is not the end of the world. One outcome of this technique may be a simple list of things you can laugh at and avoid.

Technique 2: Use some type of visual to spark your imagination. Find a magazine picture or photograph that has something to do with the problem or issue you want to address. Select a photo you are unfamiliar with and note anything you see that might give you several different perspectives about what is happening in the picture. For example, George M. used this technique recently to see if he could get a new perspective about a morale problem in his work group. In the photograph he selected, there was a young boy in a baseball uniform sitting on the ground, propped dejectedly against a cyclone fence, staring out toward left field. The sadness on the boy's face reminded George of the looks he had been seeing in his department during the past few weeks. Instead of focusing on his coworkers, he began wondering what might have happened on that baseball field. He reached several conclusions:

- The boy's team has just lost an important game. Somehow, the young player contributed to the loss and is feeling embarrassed that he has let his team down.

- This is the final game of the season and the young boy is sad because he realizes this is the last time this team of friends will ever play together.
- The boy's team is winning a championship game by five runs. The boy has made a major contribution to their success, and the manager has just taken him out of the game so that one of the backup players gets a chance to play.
- The boy's sadness has nothing to do with baseball. Something else happened earlier in the day, and he is thinking about it.

There were other items on the list, and George was soon beginning to let his mind make some interesting connections. One of the conclusions he decided to explore was the morale of one of his coworkers, which was low, because they had just finished a difficult but highly successful project together. Their collective hard work had paid off, but their task force team was about to be disbanded.

Technique 3: Ask "what if" questions. Using "what if" questions can broaden your perspective and force you to look at different sides of the problem. Suppose you are trying to clean up a backlog of old work, and you ask yourself questions like: "What if I asked some of the department managers to work the next few weekends to help our group catch up?" or "What if I asked for volunteers to give up ten minutes of their lunch time each day to help us?" or "What if I ignored most of the backlog until someone called to complain or inquire about the status of a claim?"

Some broader, more controversial questions can also stir up interesting conversations—"What if we didn't care about morale?" or "What if we walked out of meetings that were too long or too boring?" or "What if we went home when we thought we had done a fair day's work?" Of course, using "what if" questions is a technique for generating ideas and encouraging creative thinking. They are paths to a solution.

Once you begin thinking of "what if" questions, you will be surprised at the number of possibilities you can generate in a short time. Try it now with one of your current problems. Try to list at least ten questions. You may find that some new ideas begin to emerge. Do not make judgments about these ideas at this time. Just list them for future consideration.

Technique 4: Reverse thinking. Try flipping the problem around so that you are looking at it from the opposite perspective. For example, years ago, the people who were paid to increase the sale of cigarettes spent countless hours trying to determine what they could remove from cigarettes to make them safer for consumers. When someone used reverse thinking and asked instead, "What can we *add* to our product to make it safer?" the cigarette filter was created.

Dr. Edward Jenner studied hundreds of cases of smallpox trying, without success, to find the cause. Finally, he reversed his thinking and shifted his attention to people who did *not* have the disease. He discovered that dairymaids apparently were never stricken. They caught a milder disease, cowpox, which protected them from smallpox. From this discovery, Dr. Jenner developed a vaccine that defeated the deadly smallpox disease.

There is also the classic story about the woman who helped double sales for the shampoo company she worked for by adding one word—repeat—to the instructions on each product container. A London cab company once saved thousands of dollars each year in training costs for new cab drivers by reversing their thinking about an old problem. Instead of devoting weeks of classroom time to map reading and discussions about how to get from one place to another, the company decided to offer discount fares to any local customers willing to direct drivers to their destinations. This on-the-job training got the drivers out of the classroom and on to the road weeks ahead of schedule, and there was a win/win cost benefit to any customers who knew where they were going.

❖   ❖   ❖   ❖   ❖

CASE STUDY

Rosemary S. works for a small but very successful manufacturing company that is about to be acquired by one of several competing bidders. At a staff meeting today, Rosemary's manager, Ted, told her and her coworkers that they needed to eliminate as many unnecessary expenses as they could as quickly as possible. Two of the potential buyers would be discussing financial matters with the group in about eight weeks, and Ted wanted things to look as positive as they could. He asked the group to shoot for a fairly high target—30 percent reduction in expenses by the end of the year—and then he asked Rosemary to lead a brainstorming session with her coworkers.

Your Analysis

Before reviewing Rosemary's approach to this problem, take a few minutes to write down some of your ideas about this situation. What would you do and why?

_____

_____

_____

The Employee's Actions

Rosemary followed standard brainstorming procedures, and before long ideas were pouring forth from the group: have fewer group meetings; reduce the number of outgoing telephone calls; allocate a specific time each day to retrieve e-mail messages rather than check in a few times each hour; look for ways to combine jobs and spread out the work more systematically; manage supplies more efficiently; and agree as a group to be more punctual in the morning and at lunch. In about twenty minutes, Rosemary and her group had generated more than sixty ideas, including several gems that could help them significantly reduce expenses.

Then Rosemary had the idea to try reverse thinking. She challenged the group to think differently about the problem: "Instead of focusing only on reducing expenses, why don't we list some ways we might be able to increase income or cash flow?" Within minutes, the group had listed names of prospective customers who should be contacted, names of slow-paying customers who should be nudged for delinquent fees, and two major customers who should be contacted and assured that any acquisition wouldn't damage their long-term relationship with Rosemary's company.

❖ ❖ ❖ ❖ ❖

Technique 5: Lateral thinking. This is a concept developed over thirty years ago by creativity guru Edward de Bono. The basic idea is that our brains are excellent information-processing systems that allow us to make sense of the outside world. Incoming information is organized into channels or tracks. When we want to know something about a particular thing, we can follow the established channel and have ready access to all our available information about that subject. Sometimes, however, we may need to break out of those fixed channels to find new and better paths for exploration.

It is this breaking away from established patterns, this moving sideways to change concepts, that de Bono named "lateral thinking." Instead of moving steadily forward in the most obvious direction, we may be surrounded by other useful ideas that are behind us or on tracks running diagonally out from the path we are attempting to pursue. The familiar rational path moves us comfortably through known landscapes. The less comfortable lateral path takes us into new territory where we are exposed to new ideas. We move into areas of possibilities and opportunities.

Here's an example of a creative approach a group used to identify some new advertising techniques: The team leader took out a dictionary and asked a member of the group to pick a page number. The person selected page 658, and then suggested the tenth word in the left column. The magic word was "hangar," defined as a shed or shelter especially for an aircraft. The leader did not put any limits on what happened next. She simply encouraged the group to yell out their ideas, which she listed on a flipchart. Some people focused on the building itself and how the roof could be used for ads that could be seen from the air. Some people focused on new and different ways to include their advertisements in the airplane magazines. One individual decided to play around with the word "hanger" instead of going with the rest of the group and suggested a two-sided paper cover for hangers at the dry cleaners that would contain ads for fabric care products. The process generated many ideas, including several new approaches that the group could implement with very little time, energy, and cost. Of course, some of the ideas were not useful at all. But there was no criticism of the off-the-wall suggestions, and the group decided to save any ideas that might be helpful for later discussions.

Technique 6: Think outside the box. Every March, sixty-four college basketball teams participate in a national competition to determine which is the best team. It is a one-game elimination process—when a team loses, it stops competing, and only the winner advances to the next round. If you were asked to determine how many games it will take to produce that final champion, one approach would be to chart how the sixty-four original teams move toward a final four, then two, then one surviving team. These charts are often the graphic symbols used in office betting pools. You could draw these boxes of information and count the number of games that will be played. Or you could try another approach that requires a slightly different mind-set. For there to be only one winner in this competition, sixty-three teams need to lose one game. The tournament, therefore, has sixty-three games.

Technique 7: Play with words. Use metaphors and try language that is different from what you ordinarily use to approach a work problem. Use an analogy that you and your coworkers can identify with. For example: "Let's huddle and review our game plan. We have a lot of ground to cover in the next quarter if we hope to meet our goal and score a winning touchdown. We need to launch a solid offense, but first, we probably need to eliminate some of these distracting options. Let's decide now which two or three ideas we can afford to punt on."

Or try an analogy that everyone will understand: "This project has gotten too cumbersome and top-heavy. We need to prune it drastically if it's ever going to grow in the right direction. We need to cut away a lot of the deadwood and allow some of the new growth to see the light."

Use free association and look for different work combinations that might generate new approaches or ideas. For example, here is a flow of associated words that helped a new bank determine some possible policies and procedures: keeping customers—customer satisfaction—satisfaction guaranteed—guaranteed to work every time—time is money—money in the bank—bank on us for all your service needs—need help? Call us twenty-four hours a day.

Look for analogies and similarities in seemingly unrelated concepts. For example, when Victor F. thought about how difficult it was to resolve a complex problem, he compared the challenge to rolling a heavy stone up a steep hill. He saw himself pushing the rock upward, inch by inch, hoping he had enough control so that it did not roll back toward or over him. As Victor continued thinking about this scenario, he tried to decide what would help him succeed and listed several options:

- Ask for help from others, especially anyone willing and able to keep the stone rolling in the right direction.
- Look around the hill for some flat surface to prop the rock up temporarily while you regain strength, assess where you want to go next, and determine whether you need additional help.
- Find some natural block like a small but strong rock that you can use as a wedge to keep your rock from slipping back down the hill. This wedge will give you a sense of confidence and a feeling of security that what you have accomplished so far will not be easily undone.
- Get to the top of the hill and celebrate.

Technique 8: Change your usual frame of reference. Look for ways to combine different interests.

- Leonardo da Vinci had a variety of job titles ranging from architect and artist to astronomer and physicist. One of his real talents was crossing over from one discipline to another and applying ideas from one field to another. His creative genius led to one important scientific discovery after another. While we all cannot be Leonardo da Vinci, we all have the ability to bring things we learn from one discipline or experience to another.
- While many of his contemporaries chiseled figures and faces onto the marble stones of their work, Michelangelo looked at his work from a different perspective. He believed that his statues were al-

ready buried in the marble he brought into his studio and that his life's work was to free these "prisoners" for the world to see by chipping away the excess stone.

At a recent staff meeting, Amy made this observation: "Customer complaints increased by 10 percent last year. That's the highest increase we have had in over eight years. I wonder why the number was not higher? What do you think?" An interesting exchange of factors took place, and several positive action items were developed.

At another meeting, Amy stated the issue she wanted her group to address: "Let's put away our reports, charts, graphs, and statistical diagrams and talk about what our guts are telling us to do. Let's talk about how we're feeling. Let's use our instincts, our intuition, our imaginations." Although there was some initial discomfort, the group used the process effectively and later admitted that they actually had fun doing it.

Technique 9: Make believe. Start with some wishful thinking. Wouldn't it be great if our most difficult customers learned to be more courteous? Wouldn't work be more enjoyable if our managers gave us more autonomy? Wouldn't it be wonderful if we got a small financial bonus every time we beat one of our production deadlines?

Fantasize, daydream, let your mind wander over new territory. You may be surprised by what you discover.

Technique 10: Celebrate your creativity. Yell "Eureka!" Ring a bell. Pat yourself on the back or get someone else to do it for you. Send yourself flowers. Remind yourself that being creative can be fun.

Whenever you take a more creative approach to solving a problem, remember to stay focused on the positive aspects of the process. Positive thinking capitalizes on opportunities and takes advantage of the best available options. The main frame of reference is getting things done by determining what you need to do to make an idea work. It is an action-oriented, roll-up-your-sleeves approach to solving problems. It builds on possibilities and potential. It generates its own energy and empowers you to take risks. It helps you get results instead of stranding you in a "I wonder what would have happened if I had done this?" position.

On the other hand, negative thinking dwells on all the reasons why an idea will not or cannot work. It emphasizes barriers, obstacles, risks, dangers, restrictions, and objections. Although the first reaction to a possible solution might seem positive—"Yes, that could work"—it is followed immediately by all the reasons it probably should not be considered—"but we'll need more time, more money, permission from senior management, approval from the legal department, consensus from everyone in the department," or something else that makes even trying this solution too much trouble. By the time a negative thinker has listed all the reasons why an idea will not fly, it has been shot down and grounded forever.

The ultimate objective of any problem-solving activity is your ability to determine an effective, efficient, and acceptable option that removes obstacles and helps you accomplish your goals. The first part of your process involves choosing the best way to proceed.

Logical thinking uses facts, figures, and specific evidence. It is based on concrete information and not on hunches or even educated guesses. It is a systematic, sequential, and structured approach:

- Let's list and evaluate pros and cons.
- Let's make sure we understand our final objective.
- Let's see where we are so far.
- Let's summarize what we have discussed so far.

Creative thinking approaches problem-solving with an open mind and a belief that no idea is too stupid. It involves breaking with a standard approach and seeing a problem from new perspectives. There is an optimism—"The sky's the limit"—and a spirit of adventure—"Let's play around with this one for a while"—that make creative thinkers fun to be around. The search for something unique often leads to discoveries, new insights, and multiple possibilities.

Your effectiveness at solving problems can be an important component of how satisfied you are in your personal life and how successful you are at work. There is a strong connection between how you solve problems, your personal stress level, how productive you are, and how good you feel about the work you do.

8

Learn to Accept Uncertainty and Adapt to Change

Companies that learn to manage change are in the best position to take the risks needed to stay out in front.
—Michael S. Dell, founder and CEO, Dell Computer Corp.

Most people want stability and control at work, not the unpredictable new challenges often associated with downsizing, reengineering, and other initiatives designed to improve a company's productivity. The end product of these attempts to change the way a company does business is often more work with fewer people, more things to do and less time to do them, more directives and less flexibility to achieve the desired outcomes.

More than ever, you need to understand and accept why change must occur. You need to become comfortable finding out what is going on and why. You need to become skillful using the following practical techniques:

- Asking for information about changes and the potential impact of new approaches.
- Asking for help in prioritizing new assignments and redefining expectations for other tasks.
- Identifying areas where flexibility and innovation are encouraged and areas where structure and conformity are required.
- Maintaining a healthy perspective about new challenges and opportunities in your changing organization.

More than ever before, you must be receptive to change. You must be flexible and innovative; you must be able to accept uncertainty and tolerate ambiguity. In this chapter, we will examine a planning model and techniques that can help you gain and maintain control of your work life. We will focus on ways you can anticipate factors that will force you to change and understand the possible outcomes of a new or different situation and how you can manage your reaction to it.

Siuberto Socarras, Principal, Socarras Consulting Services, believes that finding comfort in an organization is no longer a healthy priority.

> I need to find comfort in my own entrepreneurial career. There will be more comfort for me there than anywhere else.
>
> One of the techniques that has helped me maintain perspective and flexibility is a willingness to experiment gradually. If an idea made sense, I tried it.
>
> Another technique I have used is to stay focused on being a more complete individual. I find I can balance work and the personal side of my life by holding a carrot out for myself. Pursuing this goal—"lead a richer, more balanced life"—helps me take more risks.
>
> We also need to be sensitive to diversity, especially in a high-tech age where information is available to everyone, young and old. Where is the wisdom we need for the future? It can come from both older and younger workers. Younger workers may have more information, more creative ideas, even though they have less actual work experience. Younger people are helping me to grow. Cultural diversity is critical. Our world is much more integrated today. There is no room anymore for prejudice and personal bias.

In times of rapid change, you will need to be able to move quickly, to anticipate where the next change may come from, and be flexible enough to change direction and try new approaches. You will need to keep your eye on things you might not have ever watched before. You will need to be alert for other opportunities and potential problems so that you can be as proactive as possible. You will need to be able to distinguish between nonessential work (often those tasks that have become more habitual than critical) and essential work (those tasks that really make a difference today).

Rob Hartwell has learned that the ability to anticipate and adapt to change is vitally important in the high-tech industries:

If you don't change and acquire new skills, you'll get left behind. The key is understanding that change is inevitable and accept it. I like to look at change as an opportunity rather than an obstacle. I believe change presents new opportunities for professional growth.

Karen DiNunzio, a management consultant who works with many Fortune 500 companies, believes that:

Dealing with change is a big struggle for most of us. It's a topic that's constantly on people's minds every second of every day. We can't predict how much change will happen in the next year. People need to keep current about what's going on in their profession, their industry, their company. People who thrive see the trends and respond to them rather than being paralyzed or concerned about them. They take the initiative to deal with what's coming along. People who are in danger of being downsized need to look for future opportunities. They may need to go out to other departments, sell themselves, network, and ask for coaching or mentoring support from their managers. They need to develop and maintain a positive mind-set. People need to be smarter about their environment and how they fit in.

When the possibility of change begins to emerge or when change actually occurs, people tend to respond in different ways:

■ Some people take a "wait and see," inactive approach. They put on blinders, ignore the situation, and hope that it will simply go away. They do not get involved and take no immediate action. Burying their heads in the sand may give them a false sense of security, which is still more comfortable than facing the reality of the new situation.

■ Some people try to deal with what is going on by bonding with others who are also affected. Commiserating with each other, they develop coping strategies to help them make the best of what they perceive as a bad situation. Rather than focus on actions to help them deal effectively with the change, they often assume a "victim" mentality and devote time and energy to resisting what is happening.

■ Some people react to change quickly once they have determined they have no choice about the situation. They take a "fire-fighting" approach to the situation and rush in with a grab bag of options and actions that might work.

Sue Strong, a senior management consultant at Hoffman-LaRoche, believes that constant change creates a reactive environment in which people often act before they think:

> People are feeling incredible stress. They are more interested in doing something, anything, than in doing the right thing. They are trying to do so much that they are missing the forest for the trees. Unrealistic workloads are creating a lack of quality, and people are allowing it to happen. The challenge is to find the time to analyze changing situations so that we can make informed decisions about how to deal with them effectively. We need to be able to understand trends and anticipate the changes that are coming. We need to be operating out of creation and not reaction.

■ Some people anticipate change and develop plans to deal with it. They are advocates of change, individuals who have taken the time to understand what is going on and why. They usually take a positive, optimistic, and creative approach to change, and try to help others see the potential benefits of new approaches.

■ Some people become paralyzed by what is going on around them. They are so frightened by change they are unable to discuss their feelings with others. Instead, they internalize their worst fears and become victims of their own self-fulfilling prophesy: "I told you this would be horrible!"

When you cannot control everything that is going on around you, focus on aspects of the situation you can control. For example, you may not be able to anticipate or manage what is happening, but you can control how you react to the situation, how you decide to deal with it, whether you let it overwhelm or defeat you, whether you confront the situation and make it better, or bury your head in the sand and make it worse.

Some people hang on to the past for as long as they can, often remembering the "good old days" with an exaggerated sense of well-being, creating a nostalgic memory that is often much better than the reality they experienced. There is a tendency to glorify the past, especially when the present is filled with uncertainty and doubt. A panic sets in when they are faced with anything new. They cling to the false memory of "better times." They stick to the old tried and true ways and resist any change that leaves them on shaky, untested ground. They dig in their heels and become antagonistic toward any changing conditions. If they would remember that in the *real* past, they dealt with real issues successfully, they might face the future with much more courage and confidence.

Change is anything that requires us to shift from the old and familiar to something that is new and different. Humorist Ogden Nash once said, "Progress might have been all right once, but it has gone on too long." In today's fast-paced, competitive marketplace, organizations must change in order to survive and prosper. Our world is changing more rapidly than ever before. Adaptability has become one of our major challenges and flexibility one of our primary work priorities. Futurist Alvin Toffler describes this phenomenon as "waves of change" that are accelerating at a faster pace and becoming less predictable than at any time in our history.

There are a number of factors affecting the nature and pace of change. In some cases, there is a ripple effect that accelerates the need for change and brings a sense of urgency to certain situations. For example:

■ Because of global competition, your organization may need to streamline processes, become "leaner and meaner," and initiate downsizing and reengineering efforts.

■ Because of recent shifts from a manufacturing to an information economy, your company may be initiating a variety of technological advances that involve new equipment and systems.

■ Because of aging facilities and equipment, your company may be taking a serious look at current locations, operations, machinery, and other resources.

■ Because new direction often requires new ideas, your company may have changed leadership, brought in new people, created new policies and procedures, and defined new ways to use limited financial resources.

Any one of these factors can create natural negative reactions. When several or more are happening, initial responses can be strong and potentially harmful. For example:

■ You may have concerns about heavier workloads, different priorities, your ability to meet new goals and expectations, the company's stability, your personal career development, and future opportunities with the company.

■ You may have anxiety about your potential loss of position, influence, or control of what is going on in your immediate work environment.

■ You may be experiencing feelings of frustration, past resentments about changes that did not work well, confusion about what is happening and why, anger that this change has to occur now, and insecurity about what to do if things get worse instead of better.

- You may just be feeling some of those natural concerns most people have when change is imminent. We all have felt fear of the unknown or fear of failure. It may also be a fear of success—what changes will I need to make if I take advantage of this new opportunity and succeed? When people succeed, they sometimes experience negative side-effects they may not have anticipated: longer work hours, less time with family, more problems to address.

Regardless of your initial reaction to the change that is occurring, you will begin to experience some emotional issues that need to be addressed or resolved before you can move forward successfully. You will probably be concerned with both continuity—those values and positive practices from the past—and change—those desired outcomes and new challenges that lie ahead. As you move from the past toward the future, you may go through a fairly tumultuous transitional state. Here are some of the issues people often identify:

- Anger, pain, grief, and resentment about the changes sometimes articulated as "Why me? Why now? Who needs this?"
- Uncertainty, inconsistency, confusion, and doubt about whether the new will be better than the old.
- Loss of identity, relationships, and control as processes and procedures get juggled or realigned.
- Need to adjust, rearrange, put things in order, and make sense of things, especially goals, roles, and responsibilities.
- The more difficult the transition becomes, the growing temptation to idealize and glorify the way things used to be and hold on to too much of the past.
- Difficulty imagining possible positive alternatives even though they may have been crystal clear earlier in the process.

All of these issues may contribute to lower morale, productivity, efficiency, and effectiveness. The challenge now is to stay focused on the ultimate benefits you will receive by moving successfully to the new desired state. There are several key transition questions that can help you get through this difficult stage:

- What's at stake for me and the company if the change does not go smoothly?
- What am I willing to give up to make this change work?
- What are the risks and opportunities associated with this change?
- What am I willing to do?

- What will my new priorities be?
- What are the potential benefits?
- What concerns do I still have about this change?
- What lessons have I learned from the past that can help me in this transition?
- What do I want in the future, and how will this change help me?

Some people hang on to the past for as long as they can, often with an exaggerated sense of well-being, creating a nostalgic memory that is usually much better than the reality they experienced. There is a tendency to glorify the past, especially when the present is filled with uncertainty and doubt. A panic sets in when they are faced with anything new. People take comfort in saying, "At least we survived those bad times and created some stability for ourselves. But how will we ever deal with these new changes, challenges, and crises?" When this type of panic sets in, many people become resistant, almost antagonistic, to changing conditions.

Instead of learning from their past experiences that they are capable of making it through hard times, they fear that they will never be able to do it again. They need to shift their focus and concentrate on ways to build the future instead of trying to defend, glorify, or duplicate the past. If they would remember that in the *real* past, they dealt with real issues successfully, they might face the future with much more courage and confidence.

When you cannot control everything that is going on around you, focus on aspects of the situation you can control. For example, you may not be able to anticipate or manage what is happening, but you can control how you react to the situation, how you decide to deal with it, whether you let it overwhelm or defeat you, whether you confront the situation and make it better or bury your head in the sand and make it worse.

To deal effectively with change, bring it down to the level of a specific outcome or course of action you or your company has decided is necessary. Since the decision to change has already been made, there is no time or need to debate why. Hopefully, there have been frequent and productive conversations about the nature and importance of this change. You know generally what end result you are trying to accomplish, although you may not know all the details, steps, and resources involved.

One of the other potential dangers for you at this time is the temptation to speed up the process and get things over with as soon as you can. That's what our society and our business culture often encourages us to do. But any change requires thoughtful and careful attention to all of the details, not just the major ones. You are trying to avoid classic Murphy's Law problems—those unexplained and uncontrollable factors that can jeopardize the more crucial parts of a project. In an environment that may be telling you to hurry up, the best thing to do now is to slow down, at least at the start of this change, and consider as many eventualities as you can. At a time when you are probably short of resources, you cannot afford to waste them. There probably is not a lot of time available for you to fix mistakes that could have been avoided or to put out fires that could have been prevented.

The more planning and preparation you do, the better your chances of success. A clear road map that leads to the final destination should include an accurate assessment of possible detours, bumpy roads, bad weather conditions, and anything else that may interfere with a smooth journey. Be optimistic that things will proceed without a hitch; be realistic that problems can occur.

Action Steps for Implementing a Change

1. Define your overall goal, your expected outcome. When you have moved successfully through the transition state, what will the future state look like? What are the desired or required results you hope to achieve?

2. Have current, adequate, and accurate information about resources (time, money, equipment, etc.) and the level of support you can expect from your manager.

3. Create a realistic incremental schedule with clear target dates. Allow some room for error. Remember that most change does not occur overnight and that you will need to make some midcourse adjustments. However, if you have done adequate preparation and contingency planning, you should be able to move comfortably forward in implementing the change.

4. Begin your scheduled plan with optimism and enthusiasm. At this point, you have probably developed a foolproof strategy and approach that will require some minimal peripheral vision to make sure you are not blindsided by something that you were unable to anticipate. These kinds of unpredictable surprises are rare, so you should feel confident that your planned change can be implemented without incident.

Monitor your progress during your transition to the new and desired state. Measure how far you have come at each step and determine how your outcome compares with your original objective. If you have established useful measurement criteria as part of your preparation stage, the task now is to apply those measures to the process you have used and the results you have achieved. There is often a temptation at this point to say,

"Well, that's close enough," when a few final adjustments might produce a better outcome. Stop only when you are satisfied with the results. Then continue to monitor what you have accomplished until you are certain that the new approach is working the way you want.

5. Your personal objective is to arrive at a satisfactory level of commitment, which is your individual decision to accept and support what is happening because it has greater potential to help you than to harm you. The benefits to your well-being outweigh the threats.

Change only occurs when there is an imbalance between the sum of certain driving forces and the sum of opposing or restraining forces. Driving forces are usually defined as opportunities, needs, requirements, motivators, incentives, or any other factors pushing you in a new direction. Restraining forces are usually defined as fears, dangers, potential problems, uncertainty, confusion, and other factors pushing you to maintain your current position. If the forces are relatively equal, you will tend to maintain the status quo. Change will not occur.

A technique called Force-Field Analysis, developed by Kurt Lewin, is especially effective when there are opposing forces or pros and cons related to situations that require changing direction, emphasis, or methodology. It can be a helpful tool for learning about your resistance to change or your reluctance to try new approaches.

Take a few minutes to try this Force-Field approach with an example from your own personal or professional life. Use the force-field analysis chart in Figure 8-1 to plot opposing forces associated with some change you are involved with or have dealt with recently. Here are some possibilities to help you get started: accepting a new job, buying a new home or car, getting married, taking on the responsibility of caring for an aging parent, being transferred to a new department, or being asked to join a special project team.

Now think about and list all the competing forces, positive and negative, pushing you in one direction or another. Once you have identified the key forces, especially those areas of resistance, it is important to identify ways to deal with them effectively so that you can minimize them and move toward the required or desired change. The two questions to ask yourself as you try this exercise are:

1. Can I do what I need to do to change? Do I have the skills, knowledge, style, ability, and competencies to do something different?

2. Do I want to make this change? What benefits, value, and positive outcomes can I expect? Am I motivated and committed to bringing this through to a satisfactory conclusion?

Figure 8-1. Force-field analysis.

Driving Forces (Pros)	*Restraining Forces (Cons)*
What must happen? What does your manager expect? What does your company expect?	What must *not* happen? What is your worst-case scenario?
What will motivate you to make an effective decision and help resolve this problem?	What obstacles are in your way? What challenges will slow you down?
What factors are you optimistic about in this situation? What are some possible positive outcomes you hope to achieve?	What factors may make the situation worse? What could happen to affect your control of the situation?
What goals, requirements, incentives, or new opportunities are encouraging you to change?	What barriers—fear, degree of difficulty, resistance—are holding you back?
Other factors:	

As you examine the driving and restraining forces, you may also want to note how you are feeling about these factors. A transition diagram (Figure 8-2) can help you chart what you can or should be doing to go from an initial negative reaction to a positive conclusion about the change. The next two case studies show how two individuals worked through their feelings by moving in a counterclockwise direction from upper left- to upper right-hand corner. Before you read how they dealt with these changes, take a few minutes to decide what you would have done.

❖　❖　❖　❖　❖

CASE STUDY

As a result of recent policy changes, Martin is required to complete much more procedural paperwork and cost justification

Figure 8-2. Transition diagram.

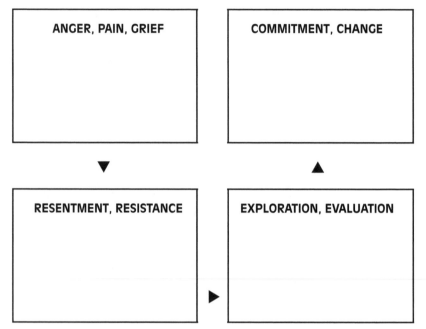

forms when requesting the resources he needs to do his job and achieve his required objectives. In the past, not only was less justification required, but the process seemed much less formal, and there weren't as many channels of approval. Martin knows that he has no choice about these new approaches, but he does want to get clarification about any areas where there may be room for flexibility.

Your Analysis

Before reviewing Martin's approach to this problem, take a few minutes to write down some of your ideas about this situation. What would you do and why?

_____

_____

_____

The Employee's Actions

Using a Transition Diagram, Martin listed the way he was feeling about this change and then dealt systematically with each factor. His graph looked like this:

Anger, Pain, Confusion	**Commitment, Change**
"I can't believe I have all this new work to do. It's unfair to expect me to do more than I am already doing. I wish they would just leave well-enough alone. I need to tell my boss I can't do it."	"I understand now that there were some major abuses and gaps in our old system. Once we eliminate them, we should be able to save the company thousands of dollars. I can certainly support that."
Resentment, Resistance	**Exploration, Evaluation**
I don't want to be a troublemaker, but I need to talk about my new priorities. I don't know what my new role is going to be."	"I'm glad I talked to my boss. Now I know more about why we had to make these changes. I think I can help."

❖   ❖   ❖   ❖   ❖

CASE STUDY

Bryn has worked for her current company for more than fifteen years. She has had the same manager, Corey, for the last five years, and has gotten along with him very well. As a result of a recent reorganization, Bryn now has a new manager, Karen, who is less experienced than her previous one. She has very different ideas about Bryn's job and her work responsibilities.

Your Analysis

Before reviewing Bryn's approach to this problem, take a few minutes to write down some of your ideas about this situation. What would you do and why?

_____

_____

_____

The Employee's Actions

Bryn used the following Transition Diagram to help her move from what was initially a negative reaction to a more positive perspective.

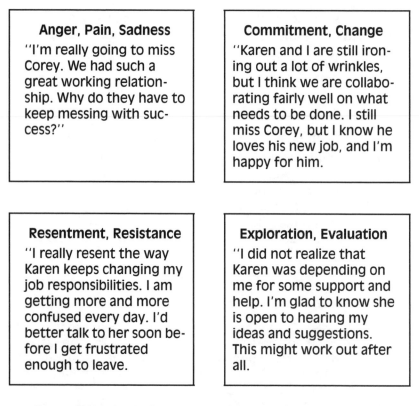

Anger, Pain, Sadness

"I'm really going to miss Corey. We had such a great working relationship. Why do they have to keep messing with success?"

Commitment, Change

"Karen and I are still ironing out a lot of wrinkles, but I think we are collaborating fairly well on what needs to be done. I still miss Corey, but I know he loves his new job, and I'm happy for him.

Resentment, Resistance

"I really resent the way Karen keeps changing my job responsibilities. I am getting more and more confused every day. I'd better talk to her soon before I get frustrated enough to leave.

Exploration, Evaluation

"I did not realize that Karen was depending on me for some support and help. I'm glad to know she is open to hearing my ideas and suggestions. This might work out after all.

Force-Field Analysis and Transition Diagrams are effective tools to help you:

- Define why change is necessary.
- Determine what the future should or must look like and why.

- Create a personal image or picture of what the desired or required future state needs to be.
- Assess your current situation in relationship to what is ideal or necessary in the future.
- Communicate openly with the right people about what must happen and why.
- Implement an effective transition process by creating a bridge between the past and the future.
- Implement specific action plans to produce the necessary change and monitor the results.

❖　❖　❖　❖　❖

There is one final reality check you can do to remind yourself that change does not have to be overly traumatic or unnecessarily difficult. Try this brief exercise to evaluate a change that has occurred in your life. Remember how you dealt with it and how you would deal with it now.

- ❏ Describe a change you have experienced in the last five years.
- ❏ Describe how you felt about this change when it first happened or when you knew it had to happen.
- ❏ Describe at least one positive outcome of the change.
- ❏ Describe at least one drawback of the change.
- ❏ Describe the key actions you took to make the change work for you.
- ❏ Describe anything you would do differently if you had to face this situation again.

When you described some of your key actions above, you may have remembered how important it was to:

- Stay focused on your short-term goals and priorities. By achieving incremental and immediate success, you built confidence and commitment to the change you were trying to implement. When helpful, you clarified any new work roles and job responsibilities.
- Minimize ambiguity and confusion by communicating messages clearly, accurately, honestly, and in a timely manner. You were not general or vague.
- Give frequent feedback to your manager and others about your progress toward goal achievements. You took calculated risks.

■ Listen more carefully than ever before. You asked questions and dealt proactively with rumors and any incorrect information. You let others know you wanted to receive information and feedback. You kept your ears open to hear the worst of what was going on before anyone else, including your manager, other departments, or your customers.

As you continue to work and try to flourish in this rapidly changing work world, remember that there are certain basic facts about change:

■ All change is not good for everyone; all change is not bad for everyone.
■ Getting angry about change usually only makes things worse.
■ Change often brings problems and stress—things may actually get worse before they get better.
■ Change often brings positive results: new methods, better tools, greater opportunities, different challenges.
■ Change is often too little, too late, and often haphazard; it is difficult to evaluate its impact fairly and objectively.
■ Change is not something someone else is supposed to make work for you—that is your job.

There are also several important strategies you can develop and implement to help you succeed. The more prepared you are for change, the better things will be for you and your company. Throughout this chapter, we have emphasized the following concepts, presented here as reminders:

❏ Take personal responsibility for anticipating and preparing for change. Show that you are willing and able to help make change happen effectively and efficiently.

❏ Take ownership of what's happening with your work and with the changes going on around you. Keep learning, keep asking questions, keep informed.

❏ Initiate changes that will improve quality, reduce costs, and save time. Be part of the solution, not part of the problem.

❏ Be professional in everything you do—demonstrate competence, confidence, and commitment. Maintain a positive outlook and a sense of humor.

❏ Shift your approaches and priorities to match the changes going on in your company. Stay current about what's going on in your company and your industry.

❐ Be a positive role model for others. Be upbeat and enthusiastic. Manage your own morale, motivation, and performance so that you can be a positive presence in your work environment.

In the next chapter, we will describe a variety of self-management techniques to help you become and stay an asset to your company.

9

Take Responsibility for Your Job Performance and Morale

Too many people put in "face time." They show up for work, and think that's good enough. Many even believe they're working hard. Most believe they're contributing.
—Judith M. Bardwick, *Danger in the Comfort Zone* (AMACOM, 1991)

Some people work just hard enough not to get fired, and some companies pay people just enough that they won't quit.
—Louis E. Boone, American educator and business writer

Today, more than ever, you need to hold yourself accountable for your own job performance. Simply putting in time and counting the hours is no longer enough. Marking off months and years of service on a retirement calendar may give you a false sense of security in today's uncertain work environment. In the current economy there are really no guarantees. "Longevity" is no longer synonymous with "loyalty." You cannot depend on others as much as you may have been able to in the past for career guidance or professional development. You can no longer rely solely on your company or your manager to "take care of you" or to guarantee you either employment or a motivating work environment. You must be able to manage your own morale, attitude, behaviors, and job performance. You must know what it will take to achieve personal satisfaction at work. In some cases, it may help to act as though you are in business for yourself. The challenge is determining how you can make a contribution to what your company is trying to accomplish. If you decide that the effort expected of you is unreasonable or too demanding, you must maintain your current level of performance until you can find what you need to regain job satisfaction—a new challenge, a new position, or a new company to hire you.

However, before you do anything drastic about leaving your current position or company, take a close look at what you can do to make your current job more challenging, interesting, and satisfying. Use the maintenance perspective checklist in Figure 9-1 to help keep things in balance. This may also be a good time to assess the status of your current job. Use the job assessment form in Figure 9-2 to think about the worst-case scenario.

There may be things you can do to bring new life to your work and at least sustain your morale while you examine and sort out other options. This is a technique that Janet L. used recently when the bank she works for instituted some radical changes to streamline the way they handled customers:

> I started out as a teller in my neighborhood branch office. I enjoyed the hours, and I really liked interacting with most of my customers. A few years later, the bank encouraged several of us tellers to take on some customer service activities. I was flattered that I was chosen. I went for some training and then sat at one of the office desks opening accounts and taking care of routine transactions. It was fun, and I even earned a little more money.
>
> A few months ago, the bank asked me to take on even more desk time by working with customers on loan applications or investment inquiries. At first, this seemed overwhelming to me. Even with some excellent training, I did not feel confident dealing with the intimate financial needs of people I have known as customers for at least ten years. I made up my mind that it was time for me to make a change, and I talked to my manager about transferring to another position in the bank. She encouraged me to give these new responsibilities a try while I considered other options. Since our conversation, I have taken my manager's advice seriously. I work at the customer service desk more than four hours each day, and I am beginning to realize that my customers trust me and appreciate my help. However, I am more certain than ever that I do not want to do this for a long time. I

(text continues on page 166)

Figure 9-1. Maintaining perspective (checklist).

Three Most Positive Aspects of Current Job	Level of Importance
1.	❒ Critical ❒ Very Important ❒ Important ❒ Nice to Have
2.	❒ Critical ❒ Very Important ❒ Important ❒ Nice to Have
3.	❒ Critical ❒ Very Important ❒ Important ❒ Nice to Have
Three Most Negative Aspects of Current Job	Level of Impact
1.	❒ Demoralizing ❒ Detrimental ❒ Bearable but not desirable ❒ Distracting
2.	❒ Demoralizing ❒ Detrimental ❒ Bearable but not desirable ❒ Distracting
3.	❒ Demoralizing ❒ Detrimental ❒ Bearable but not desirable ❒ Distracting

I would describe my job as:
❒ Better than most   ❒ Worst than most
❒ Worth keeping   ❒ Beyond my ability to fix or improve

Figure 9-2. Job assessment form.

1. Worst-Case Scenario	How likely is it to occur?	Potential impact on you:
	❒ Inevitable	❒ Devastating
	❒ Probable	❒ Significant
	❒ Possible	❒ Important
	❒ Unlikely	❒ Moderate

What actions can you take now to prevent or minimize what is happening? _____

2. Workable Alternative	❒ Long shot	❒ Better than nothing
	❒ Possible	❒ Temporary option
	❒ Depends on support from others	❒ Sign that company wants to help
	❒ Unlikely	❒ Gives me time to make other changes in current job or future career

What actions can you take now to move things closer to a workable conclusion? _____

3. Best-Case Scenario	❒ Very long shot	❒ Ideal—I keep my job and have new challenges
	❒ Possible, but not for a long time	❒ Depends on the level of commitment from the company and how long it might take to make adjustments
	❒ Department managers will need to do frequent evaluations of this new approach	❒ Gives me more positive reasons to hang in and help influence our new approach
	❒ Unlikely now that certain changes have been made	❒ Provides data for me to make an educated decision about my future
		❒ Gives me time to make other changes in current job or future career

have begun to contact other departments in the bank, and I have even talked to a local accounting company that may need some help later this year. I feel that I am doing a good job for the bank and its customers, that I am being fair by keeping my manager informed about my job search activities, and that I am maintaining a positive attitude about my work during this time of change.

This approach is one of the cornerstones of a broader strategy to keep in mind when your company changes directions, objectives, or structure. It is a proactive, not a "go with the flow," reaction to what you can do to manage your own performance and morale. Here are a few techniques to consider:

- Do your best to meet time, quality, quantity, and cost requirements. Even as things around you change, it is your responsibility to keep your work moving along at a steady, predictable pace. You may need to interact with others who can help you with the resources you need. You may need to keep others informed about new and unexpected obstacles or bottlenecks. The key point is, more than ever, to take responsibility for what is going on with your job and work hard to keep things moving in the right direction.

- Adjust well to changing priorities. You need to be able to shift from tasks that are comfortable, habitual, and easy to whatever activities will help you meet your new priorities. It may be difficult for you to let go of routine actions that you have been doing for such a long time they are now comfortable, almost second-nature practices. The need to change your approach to accommodate your changing priorities can be both a difficult and an exciting opportunity. Only you can determine which perspective to take.

- Take the initiative in developing creative solutions to problems and do what is necessary to get the job done. There may be opportunities during periods of rapid change to use the rational and creative problem-solving skills described in Chapters Six and Seven of this book. Remember that the logical approach often requires more time than the innovative approach. Therefore, decide which is the better option—a thoughtful, analytical, data-based approach that builds to some informed and tested conclusions—or an intuitive, creative, gut-feeling approach based on brainstorming and other imaginative techniques. Your ultimate objective, of course, is to get the job done. In today's fast-paced environments, a creative solution may be the better choice. Getting things under control may buy you some time to give the problem more thorough and thoughtful attention.

■ Be aggressive in dealing with emergencies. If you have not been able to anticipate or prevent an emergency from occurring, shift into your best fire-fighting behavior until you get things back under control. Don't panic and don't be tempted to point fingers, blame others, or push the crisis off on someone else. Just get busy bringing things back under control. You will have time later to analyze what happened and to determine what you can do to prevent future events like this one.

■ Accept responsibility for your work and for the consequences of your work efforts. Accountability is an important concept in most organizations today. Companies and their managers are looking for people who are willing to step up to their jobs and accept responsibility for whatever happens, even if the results are not as positive as they may have been in the past. In times of rapid, unpredictable change, doing the best you can is a fair expectation. Accepting responsibility when things fall short of your manager's expectations or your own personal standards is the first step in learning how to make things better.

Regardless of how you are feeling about the changes going on within your company, do your best to maintain a high level of personal motivation. When organizations downsize or reengineer, they often overlook, at least temporarily, some of those job factors that are extremely important to you. For example, goals, expectations, and priorities may not be as clearly defined. Instead of waiting for the company to find the time to issue new guidelines, this can be an excellent opportunity for you to initiate some personal action plans. Here are a few things you can do:

■ Set high performance standards for yourself. You know what you are capable of doing, and you know how much time and energy you are willing to invest in your changing job position. Once you have defined your own performance expectations and made certain they meet at least the minimum required by your company at this time, you should be able to proceed with a sense of confidence.

■ Do your best to foster cooperation and teamwork with others. More than ever, this may be the best time to collaborate with those key people in your Circle of Influence. You are all probably in the same boat right now, trying to figure out how things are going to develop and stabilize. Some of your colleagues may have figured out approaches that can help you. Some of them may be able to benefit from your ideas. This may also be a good time to look at your Circle of Influence to see if you need to make any adjustments. Has anyone left, become discouraged, or given into negative feelings about the future? Are there new people, not currently in your circle, who can make a positive contribution to your efforts and deserve to be included on your list of "right people?" Are there people, including your manager, who might need special help from you to keep everything in perspective for a while?

- Maintain a high level of enthusiasm and an optimistic perspective about work challenges. Even if you feel that what your company has done or is doing is not in your best interest, you need to keep your end of the bargain by working as conscientiously and efficiently as possible. You need to set an example for others while you decide what course of action you want to pursue to meet your new work expectations or look for a different position.

There are several things you can do to manage your current job and improve your personal performance:

- Focus on a specific goal. What do you need or want to accomplish by when? Set a challenging short-term goal for yourself. Once you have defined your target, move forward with a strong sense of purpose.

- Keep track of your own performance. Pay attention to things you are doing well. When you make a mistake, look for lessons and begin using what you have learned. Do not dwell on the errors. Look at your successes and build on them. Maintaining the right balance can minimize your level of stress.

- Strive for excellence even if no one else seems to notice. Take personal pride in your own good work.

- Learning new skills and behaviors takes time, effort, and patience. It is normal to feel uncomfortable during times of change. If you stay optimistic about the value of these new techniques or this different approach, you will be able to achieve a satisfactory level of confidence and competence.

- Once you and your supervisor have discussed and clarified your work requirements, set your own performance standards to meet or exceed these expectations. Then stop comparing your performance with anyone else's. You are, in effect, managing your own performance and your own work outcomes. Even if the new job is not perfect, do whatever you can to make it better.

Karen DiNunzio encourages her clients that they are in charge of themselves. Here are a few steps she suggests to help you take control of your work life:

- Become aware of where you are not taking responsibility now. Many of us have become comfortable with a false sense of dependency that our companies have created for us over the years.

- Become aware of places where you need to take more responsibility, especially areas where you may need to take greater risks.
- Keep a journal of your efforts to take control of your work and manage your morale.
- Note how behavior changes have helped.
- Track your progress, especially your successes.
- Study new ways to continue taking responsibility for your actions, behaviors, and attitudes.

Of course, in order to maintain control of your job and manage your own performance, you need the help and support of others. Your success will depend on your ability to:

- Access and apply information, especially any new data, technical knowledge, or procedural guidelines that affect your goals, priorities, and work practices.
- Secure and use necessary resources, especially money, time, materials, and support personnel.
- Get and maintain endorsement and support from your managers and others who can give you encouragement and recognition.
- Maintain a high level of self-esteem and accept responsibility for the job you are being paid to do. The challenge is to determine whether you believe what you are doing is still relevant or useful. Are you still adding value to your company? Does your company still believe your contribution is worth your salary?

The more you take responsibility for your own actions and your own morale, the more you will be able to apply your talents to tasks that will help you succeed. You have both the opportunity and responsibility to manage your own destiny. In *The Empowered Manager*, Peter Block describes empowerment as "an act of faith. We commit ourselves to operate in a way that we believe in because it is what we have to do. Other people's experience may act as signposts for us, but we take the trip alone."

Others will have an impact on your efforts, but you are ultimately in charge. By keeping the proper perspective about what is going on today, you will be more alert and ready for tomorrow's opportunities.

The best way to get and keep a balanced perspective about your work is to compare the positive aspects of your job to the negative aspects. For example, your list of positives might include:

- I make enough money to provide a good life for my family.
- I have been assigned to several interesting projects this year, and I have enjoyed the challenge.

- I like most of the people I work with on a daily basis, including my manager.

On the other hand, list some of the current negatives of your job. For example:

- I do not like the end-of-the-month deadlines and the overtime required to get the work done on time.
- I am not sure my manager appreciates my good work. We have a good relationship, but he rarely compliments me or gives me any kind of recognition.
- I am not certain about future career options or opportunities with my company. I want to move into other positions, but I'm not sure there is or will be anything available for me.

Once you have listed as many positives and negatives as you can think of, do a comparative assessment of your job. This is a good time to be brutally honest with yourself. If the positives outweigh the negatives, focus on ways you might be able to use those factors to improve some of the negative aspects. Often, a positive outlook can help you find a solution to some of the problems that have become part of your new job. Maintaining an optimistic, upbeat frame of mind about the things that are going well can sometimes help you keep a realistic perspective about areas that can be improved.

If, however, the negatives significantly outweigh the positives, it may be time for you to examine your situation more carefully. You may have identified some insurmountable obstacles or problems that will require a thoughtful response from you. This is a good time to talk to members of your Circle of Influence—especially to anyone you know who has experienced and survived what you are going through. It is also an excellent time to discuss with your manager any strategies you can implement to bring some equilibrium back into your job. The worst thing you can do is panic, get angry, assume that nothing can be done, and leave. The best thing you can do is to continue doing the best job you can while you talk to key people, see what positives you can leverage to reduce some of the negatives, implement some remedial actions, and stay in your current job for at least six months to see if you can implement any changes. During that six-month period, start taking some precautionary steps—polish up your resume, begin networking both inside and outside your company, read everything you can about job opportunities within your industry, and talk to others who have chosen completely different work options, like self-employment. This careful, thoughtful, proactive approach is a way for you to examine your options as you continue to maintain perspective about what is happening with your work and your career. If you decide that you need to move to another position, we will examine in the next chapter some strategies and techniques to help you manage that process and transition.

On a more positive note, however, consider how Ali S. resolved what had become a major work issue for her—one that had caused her to begin thinking about leaving.

❖   ❖   ❖   ❖   ❖

CASE STUDY

Despite a number of positive things going on in her sales and marketing position, Ali began to notice that she was being passed over for the more challenging work assignments and for the promotions that often come with these special projects. At a recent meeting, Ali also noticed that her manager actually gave someone else in the department credit for her hard work. Ali got no recognition, not even a thank-you, for a major contribution she had made to her department and her company. In spite of her best efforts to maintain a positive perspective, Ali was very angry about this negative aspect of her job. Her first thought was to leave the meeting so that her manager would get the message that she was angry. However, one of the remaining agenda items was a major project with a new customer, TAMEC Electronics. Ali wanted to see if she would be assigned to the project.

Twenty minutes later, Ali had been assigned a minor role on the new project team. As the meeting adjourned, several co-workers came up to her and commiserated with her about how unfair the company was, how the "glass ceiling" was keeping qualified women and minorities in the lowest job positions, and how they could not wait to walk out some day and let the company discover the talent it had lost. Ali thanked them for their comments and went to look for a quiet place to plan her next moves.

Your Analysis

Before reviewing Ali's approach to this problem, take a few minutes to write down some of your ideas about this situation. What would you do and why?

The Employee's Actions

Despite the strong encouragement from her coworkers to point fingers at the company or blame her manager, Ali put those options aside and began a more personal self-assessment. First, she sketched out on paper the special requirements of the TAMEC project. The routine tasks were easy. They were the ones she would have major responsibility for—billing, requisitions, follow-up telephone calls, orchestrating outside tours, and status reports about new or obsolete projects. It was a good list of activities that Ali would enjoy doing, would do well, and would probably not get any credit for accomplishing. So one of Ali's first questions was, "How do I make sure the right people know about my contributions without making it seem like I'm bragging or tooting my own horn?"

Next, Ali sketched unique tasks associated with the TAMEC project. There were many varied requirements that would be a part of this important contract, things like daily contact with their marketing department about sales calls and new prospects; regular meetings with their production team about product complaints; and instant e-mail updates about any changing demographics. As Ali compared the two lists, she began to realize there were some connections between the distribution and the unique task requirements. Additionally, she noticed a few places where she could serve as a bridge between other project team members, occasions where her information would help others. Ali decided to discuss those areas with her manager, offer her help and support, and emphasize the value of streamlining several of these processes. She believed he would accept her approach. As she prepared for the meeting, she also decided to document every idea, suggestion, and contribution she would make to this project—a copy for herself and a summary reminder for her manager. Finally, Ali decided that if her manager noticed her contribution and passed on even the slightest compliment, she would find time soon to broach the subject of a promotion based on her past and recent performance.

❖   ❖   ❖   ❖   ❖

Tina Hartwell believes:

> You have to take responsibility for your own success. You need to take control. If you don't, someone else will. If you want your job to evolve, you can always contribute to bigger projects and new assignments.

However, if you find things are more out of your control than you imagined, you may need to find different personal motivators to help you stay positive while you regain balance in your job or make the necessary arrangements to leave. Dorothy Meyers describes some of the factors she depends on:

> My life consists of a large percentage of positive and stress-reducing outlets. I have a lot of positive outlets in my life—hobbies, crafts, positive people, prayer, laughter, gardening, cheerleaders on the outside who help me. I measure success by how I am viewed by my family. I already feel successful, but I want to stay challenged and excited by what I am doing. So success also depends on how much change I can incorporate into my life.

There are two familiar and tested processes that can help you achieve a balanced perspective during these times of turbulent change. The first concept is called "The Self-Fulfilling Prophesy." In its simplest form it states that what you believe will happen—good or bad—probably will happen. If you can imagine only terrible things for yourself, you most likely will set yourself on a path of disappointment, anxiety, and failure. If you believe that things are bad now but that they can get better, you will operate from a position of optimism that can lead you along a constructive path to positive outcomes.

The second proactive approach you can use to help keep things in perspective is called "Positive Self-Talk." It is like the adult version of the childhood classic *The Little Engine That Could*. In this children's book, the train's constant affirmations of "I think I can, I think I can" eventually bring it to the top of the hill. A similar type of positive talk can help you get where you need or want to be. The best approach is to start with statements that can lead you to small successes: "If I do this task, I will

accomplish this outcome by the end of the month. I know I can do it."
With this initial achievement, you can continue to build toward greater
accomplishments, even if you need to deal with obstacles or barriers. For
example, your next piece of self-talk might sound like this: "I did not
expect to have this much resistance from the accounting department, but
if I stick to my guns, I think I can convince them that my approach will
help."

Finally, Positive Self-Talk is not a way for you to talk yourself into
unrealistic conclusions. If you are truly unhappy with your current job,
and you know for sure it will never get better, your self-talk—still positive—might sound like this: "I need to talk to someone in human resources about what other opportunities might be available to me. I need
to call on my network of friends and business associates to see if they have
any suggestions. Meanwhile, I need to continue doing my best work here
so that, if and when I need to go, my performance record is a positive
one."

Whenever you feel you are losing perspective about your job, take a
step back and assess the situation as objectively as you can. This is not
always easy to do, especially if you are having emotional reactions to the
situation. The job assessment form in Figure 9-2 can help give you a quick
snapshot of what is happening.

1. Start at the top by stating your worst-case scenario. What is the
last thing you would want to happen in this situation at this time? What
are you most afraid of and why? How likely do you think it is that the
worst could happen? What can you do to prevent it from happening or to
prepare yourself for when it does?

For many people, the upper left box of the Job Assessment form
contains comments like:

- I might lose my job.
- I might be transferred to another department.
- I might be removed from this project team and assigned to one I
  will not like.

If you need to use this form, check off the boxes about how likely
this scenario is to occur and how much impact it will have on you.

2. For now, skip the action steps box and move down the form to
"A Workable Alternative." For many people, this box includes comments
like:

- I might be able to keep my job until the company sorts out priorities and resolves any problems.

- If I get transferred, I might wind up in a department that I like better than this one.
- If I get reassigned to another project team, I might meet new people with talents I can learn from.

3. At the bottom of the form, list your best-case scenario. Be honest with yourself. You probably will never again be able to say, "Things will return to the way they used to be, and I will work until retirement doing exactly what I have always done."

For many people, this lower left box includes comments like:

- I might be able to bring some of my best skills and experiences to this new function in a way that will help the company succeed.
- As long as the company is willing to ask for my ideas, I might be able to make some suggestions that can help.
- There may be some opportunities here that I need to evaluate more closely.

Once you have completed the charting part of this form, it is time to focus on the action planning boxes. At first, your plans might sound like, "What can I do to avoid imminent disaster?" But if you stay as positive as you can about your options, you might begin to see some hopeful signs as you move down the page. The key thing to focus on is what you need to do to regain or maintain your level of satisfaction at work. The objective is not to salvage your current job or modify it so that it approximates what you need or want. This may be the best opportunity you have ever had to review what work you like to do, how well you do it, and how willing you are to continue doing more of the same or start doing more of something new. The best way to evaluate your interests, skills, and accomplishments is to look at your most recent performance reviews—the formal ones you and your manager have done or the informal ones you have done for yourself as a way of keeping track of your own performance.

These periodic reviews provide the day-to-day links between the goals and priorities you set at the beginning of the year and the formal performance review at the end of the year. Although you will want your manager to share these reviews with you, there are several things to do to prepare for these important conversations. Also, you should review your own performance simply as a self-assessment to see how you are doing with your current goals and priorities.

The key to keeping track of your performance is the ability to recognize and analyze *what* you have achieved (results) and *how* you have or are achieving those results (process). As you review both results and process, you will reach one of the following conclusions:

- Results and process are both acceptable (or better).
- Results are acceptable (or better), but process needs improvement.
- Results are not quite acceptable, but process seems to be working.
- Both results and process could be better.

Whenever you review your goals and priorities and do a self-assessment of your performance, take into consideration:

- The specific results you have achieved in relation to your priorities
- Goal achievement to date—what have you done so far and what is left to do
- Needed revisions to goals or priorities to reflect changing conditions
- An honest progress assessment so that you have accurate data to share with your manager or other key people
- Any plans to change your current activities or modify your performance

Your personal review should balance the concern for results and process. Reviewing results is relatively straightforward if the goal has been documented in measurable terms. The difficult area for most people is objectively assessing *how* the results are being achieved. This is when you need to think carefully about performance quality issues like the skills, knowledge, behaviors, methods, techniques, and personal practices employed. This is usually not an easy task for you to do on your own. You may want to ask for feedback from someone you trust if you have any concerns about a particular area of performance. Notice in the following examples how these employees reviewed their own progress on key goals:

One of Lauren B.'s priority objectives is to implement by December 31 of this year a method of maintaining all equipment that will eliminate 95 percent of current unplanned down time. When she recently reviewed her performance, she set up a checklist to chart her progress and her level of satisfaction with this assignment. The completed form looked like this:

Results:	Acceptable or better. Currently one month ahead of schedule with only two major obstacles ahead.
Process:	Support from other departments has been timely and helpful. I need to figure out a

	way to expedite the reporting process from our software designers. I need to schedule a meeting with them. This is a to-do list item for next week.
Performance Qualities:	I think I did some damage to my relationship with the information technology manager. I may have moved too quickly to implement an idea he should have had a chance to review and approve. I need to rebuild the important bridge we have always had. I will call him tomorrow.
Personal Satisfaction:	I am really enjoying this project. It has been both challenging and rewarding. I have gotten some positive feedback from my manager. I am optimistic that this objective will be a success story for me, my department, and the company. I would like to be assigned to similar projects in the future.

This assessment provided Lauren with a quick view of the project, its status, and where she needs to sharpen her approach. She can also use this data as part of her ongoing conversations with her manager.

Richard S. faced a different type of challenge when he did a midyear review of one of his objectives: to deliver to manufacturing a prototype of a water processing filter that meets all specifications designated in the executive memo dated 4/9/98. The prototype should be provided by September 6, 1999 for testing in early December 1999.

When Richard reviewed his performance, he found some significant problems and charted them immediately. His completed form looked like this:

Results:	Despite several meetings with production managers from manufacturing, the product specifications are still not completely defined. There were several surprise changes at the last meeting, and I need to meet one-on-one with at least two of the managers to convince them that we are beginning to fall behind schedule. I will lay out a plan for discussion and probably ask them to go to lunch with me some day

next week. After the three of us have talked, I will note the changes we agreed to on the original executive memo and discuss it with my boss so that he is not surprised or blind-sided at one of his meetings. I will also give him a status report showing that I am about three weeks behind schedule and slightly under budget. If I can get and maintain cooperation from some of the production managers, I should be able to meet this objective.

Process: My own design work has been complicated to some degree by other department managers wanting to make suggestions and modifications. I have learned to be more assertive with them about my own needs, and we have reached agreement about how and when to review their ideas. I feel that I am more in control than before, but I have learned that on future projects, I will need to set some ground rules earlier in the process.

Performance Qualities: I think I assumed that people knew my time and budget constraints. I realize now that some of the key people I needed for support were unaware of the scope and significance of my objectives. They were busy with their own priorities, and I should have been communicating with them more directly, clearly, and quickly.

Personal Satisfaction: I feel that I am working harder than I should be to bring this project to a satisfactory conclusion. I do not like the long hours—especially since most of them could have been avoided. I am not certain that this is the kind of objective I want to commit to again, and I am beginning to wonder if it's time to explore another type of career option. For now, I need to focus on completing this project, but it's time for me to begin keeping my eyes and ears open for new opportunities.

In both of these scenarios, the employees took responsibility for their job performance and morale. Lauren will probably stay in her current position for a while and seek additional challenges. Richard, on the other hand, seems to have peaked in his present position and will likely begin focusing attention on his next career move. He will assess his own skills, talents, interests, and personal aspirations. He will take steps to manage his own development and begin moving toward a more satisfactory position.

If, or when, you find yourself in a similar situation, there are techniques, tools, and approaches you can use to identify your development needs, create a plan to address those needs, and investigate growth opportunities for yourself. These activities are the subject of the next chapter.

10

Stay Current and Manage Your Own Career

In the world of the future, the new illiterate will be the person who has not learned to learn.
> —Alvin Toffler

Make every decision as if you owned the whole company
> —Robert Townsend, former president, Avis-Rent-a-Car, Inc.

In a knowledge-based economy, the new coin of the realm is learning. Learn more now, earn more in the future.
> —Robert B. Reich, former United States Secretary of Labor

In today's highly competitive workplace, you will have more responsibility than ever before for your own continuous improvement, your own professional development, and your own career. Although your manager and other company resources will want to be helpful, they may be facing some of the same challenges and concerns you are confronting. There may be a variety of reasons why they cannot be as supportive as they used to be or would like to be now:

- Perhaps their own jobs have been changed so dramatically that they have little or no time available to coach you about your professional development.
- Maybe they feel so vulnerable and threatened by company changes that they are primarily worried about their own job security.

- If your company has made radical operational changes, your manager may need time to figure out exactly what functions have expanded, stayed the same, or been eliminated.
- There may be more vigorous organizational pressure to make sure the work gets done. It will be up to you to stay current by learning new and better ways to do your job so that you continue to make appropriate contributions to your company's objectives.

Of course, there will be times during your professional development process when you will need and want to get help from your manager. There will be times when you may need to rely on others in your company for career guidance or direction. However, you have primary responsibility for these activities. More than ever, they are within your control, and you now have an exciting opportunity to manage your own career.

In this chapter, we will focus on techniques to help you close the loop you opened at the beginning of this book. We will look at ways to examine your current job and decide whether it is meeting your needs. We will review options of expanding or modifying your work to make it more satisfying, and we will consider a variety of professional development options available to help you improve your skills, knowledge, and competence in your current position or develop new competencies for your next career move.

Siuberto Socarras recently made a decision to do something different to keep himself challenged.

> Part of my self-development plan includes being flexible, learning to go with the flow, monitoring how I communicate with others. My biggest challenge right now is balancing my family, my work, and my song-writing interests. Those are my priorities, in that order. The challenge for me is to continue to take risks and leverage all of my aptitudes and skills.

While you are assessing your own level of job satisfaction and making decisions about whether it is time for you to try something new, be sure to define your next steps in ways that are consistent with the way you want your work to fit into your life. The following action steps can provide a frame of reference as you get started:

- Stay up to date on technology, industry trends, customer needs, and any other factors that are important to your personal and professional self-development.

■ Upgrade your knowledge and skills in ways that are consistent with your own future interests and career development.

Managing your own career means that you are more responsible than ever for your own continuous improvement and self-development. In this increasingly competitive world, you will be expected to identify the competencies, the knowledge, and behaviors necessary to improve performance in your current job and to prepare for future changes. You should review your own development needs periodically to ensure that you are making the maximum contribution you can to your company. However, you should also make sure you are meeting your own personal and professional goals.

Sue Strong has developed a six-step process that works for her in managing her own career:

1. Know that you need to do it, and then get started.
2. Talk to someone you trust.
3. Don't let yourself get pulled into someone else's reality.
4. Know what is really important to you—those foundational pieces like your values, your family, and your personal priorities.
5. Be clear about your own needs and personal boundaries.
6. Develop a learning attitude.

The purpose of a personal development review is to identify any performance gaps or needs. The desired outcomes are:

■ Clarity about your current strengths and any areas for improvement
■ Realistic alternatives and activities to enhance your current skills and develop new ones
■ Short-term improvement goals focused on your current job
■ Long-term improvement goals focused on future interests
■ Specific action plans for implementation and approval by your manager

Development discussions with your manager usually focus on your current job—existing requirements, new dimensions, changing priorities, potential challenges, or expansion of responsibilities within the current position. The key questions you should consider and be prepared to discuss include:

■ What technical components of your role do you need to develop to ensure that your knowledge, skills, and techniques are as current and effective as possible?

- What areas of interpersonal effectiveness or teamwork do you need to modify or improve?
- Which competencies do you need to develop to ensure continued success or to improve goal achievement in this role?

An effective way for you to start thinking about your own development needs is to ask yourself, "What is your unique contribution or individual value to the organization? What do you need to do to improve your current job performance and prepare for future roles? What new behaviors or performance attributes can you bring to your job to make you a more valuable contributor?" These are strategic questions that will help you focus on the most important role competencies you need.

Performance development is usually divided into two parts—identification of needs and action planning. Based on periodic performance reviews, the annual performance appraisal, and ongoing discussions about your interests, preferences, and aspirations, you and your manager should collaborate to:

- Identify areas where you should take action to maintain, improve, or enhance your current performance.
- Determine ways for you to get the knowledge, skills, or experience you need to prepare for future assignments.
- Create an action plan to address these needs and the development areas that you have identified. A good development plan is economical, flexible, and measurable.

There are many options available, and each can be considered to help you develop your performance. Often the best solution is a combination of options, designed specifically to meet your individual needs.

When considering available options, the following broad categories may be useful:

Job Enrichment

Changing the job itself can often enable you to develop new competencies. Job enrichment usually involves adding a new dimension to your job, such as making a presentation, writing letters and reports, participating in or leading a task force, or coaching a new employee.

Another very effective method of job enrichment is to encourage your manager to increase your visibility by involving you in higher-level meetings, assigning you to a special project team, or increasing the amount of contact you have with key customers. In this respect, job enrichment can expand your responsibilities in a way that develops existing knowledge and skills and gives you new challenges.

Job Rotations (Lateral Moves)

If properly planned, a temporary assignment can offer you the chance to demonstrate behaviors or skills that you are not able to use in your current role. Rotations generally involve some type of job change that supports the strategic needs of your organization, the operational needs of your department, and your own individual development needs. For example, spending time in another department or participating on a cross-functional team can help you learn new skills, improve your productivity, and make your job more challenging. In addition, job rotations provide your company with greater flexibility, a better match between talented employees and job requirements, and new expertise in needed areas.

A job rotation can include either a temporary assignment of a defined length or a transfer to a new position that does not involve a return to your previous job.

Formal Training

Although this type of development removes you from your workplace, it can be extremely effective if it is:

- Targeted at real needs.
- Focused specifically on identified knowledge, skills and behavior gaps.
- Reinforced by formal or informal coaching at the workplace to help you transfer new knowledge, apply new skills, and integrate new behaviors.

Self Study

You can initiate your personal and professional development by taking classes on your own time, which may lead to a professional certification, a diploma, or an advanced degree. If you have a particular career goal in mind, make sure that the training program or educational courses you plan to pursue will help you achieve that goal.

Other self-study activities such as books, tapes, and computer programs can add to your knowledge base and are less time-consuming ways to address your professional development needs. You also have greater control of the cost and time involved.

The second part of development planning involves creating an action plan to meet your needs. It should answer the following operational questions for each activity you intend to act on:

1. What will be done?
2. Where will it be done?
3. How will it be done?
4. When will it be done?
5. How much time will it take?
6. How much will it cost?
7. What must you do? What must others do?
8. How will you know when it has been done satisfactorily?

There are many ways you can manage your own continuous improvement. Use the continuous improvement worksheet form in Figure 10-1 to help you determine the best ways to proceed with your own development. In addition to some of the options mentioned earlier in this chapter, here are some others you may want to consider and discuss with your manager:

- On-the-job training
- Working on a team
- Being delegated a new task or responsibility
- Visiting customers
- Attendance at special company or professional meetings
- Special project or task force assignment in addition to current, normal workload
- Visits to other companies
- Cross-training and exposure to other departments
- Membership in professional associations

Do not be limited by the above list—think open-mindedly and imaginatively! Then, whatever development options you select, monitor the plan and be sure it is addressing the needs you have identified. There is an old German proverb that says, "What's the use of running if you're not on the right road?" A development plan will keep your continuous improvement efforts going in the right direction.

Karen DiNunzio feels that you can be successful at your price.

Be clear about where you are going and what you are willing to do to get there. The job market is tight enough that people can ask for what they need: "I can only do a good job if you give me these things." If you have a positive morale and positive confidence in your ability and skills, your manager will do as much as possible to help you succeed. Learn to balance life with work. Develop a map that shows a successful life and how your work fits into it.

Figure 10-1. Continuous improvement worksheet.

There is really no insurmountable barrier save your own inherent weakness of purpose.

—Ralph Waldo Emerson

Think about how you want to improve your job performance, develop new competencies, or acquire additional information that will help you in your current job.

Development Need	Method	Justification
Skill, Knowledge, Behavior, Competency	Resource, Technique, Learning Opportunity, or Activity	Critical? Urgent? Cost-Effective?

Because you own your career, you are primarily responsible for your own development. Your manager can play an important supportive role discussing your objectives, the company's needs, and the match between what you want and actual opportunities that are available. If you have a comfortable relationship with your manager, you may want to ask questions such as the following:

- Are my personal interests realistic? Why or why not?
- If I am interested in moving up in the organization, what do you think is the best next step for me and when? What about after that?
- Are there some cross-functional jobs that I should consider? Are there other jobs that would be a logical step in my progression?
- Do you know about any changes that might jeopardize my current position?

The objective of this type of discussion is to provide an opportunity for your manager to learn about your personal interests, give you an honest assessment of your potential to move into other job areas or assignments, reinforce your current strengths that will help you in future opportunities, and encourage continuous improvement in areas where you need developmental efforts. Of course, by the time you have this type of conversation with your manager, you should have a clear idea about the work you want to do or the position you want to have three years from now, as well as some ideas about what it will take for you to get where you want to be. The key question is: What are you currently doing to manage your own career?

If you are just beginning to get serious about this aspect of your life, the following tools and techniques may be helpful. Start by developing an overall action plan. A career worksheet like the one shown in Figure 10-2 can help you identify obstacles and gaps. Start at the bottom with your current job, and work your way toward the top, the future position you want. Use the following questions to help you determine where you are, where you want to be, and what you need to do to prepare for your next opportunity:

- What are you doing now, and how is your current job helping you prepare for the future?

- Describe as specifically as you can exactly what you want your next job to be. Define as many duties and responsibilities as you can.

- Why do you want that job? Is it something you would do well? Is it something you would enjoy doing? Would you be satisfied coming to work each day to this job?

Figure 10-2. Career worksheet.

Use the following questions to help you determine where you are, where you want to be, and what you need to do to prepare for your next opportunity:

```
┌─────────────────────────────────────────────────────────────┐
│                                                               │
│                                                               │
└─────────────────────────────────────────────────────────────┘
```

What are you doing now, and how is your current job helping you prepare for the future?

```
┌─────────────────────────────────────────────────────────────┐
│                                                               │
│                                                               │
└─────────────────────────────────────────────────────────────┘
```

Describe as specifically as you can exactly what you want your next job to be. Define as many duties and responsibilities as you can.

```
┌─────────────────────────────────────────────────────────────┐
│                                                               │
│                                                               │
└─────────────────────────────────────────────────────────────┘
```

Why do you want that job? Is it something you would do well? Is it something you would enjoy doing? Would you be satisfied coming to work each day to this job?

```
┌─────────────────────────────────────────────────────────────┐
│                                                               │
│                                                               │
└─────────────────────────────────────────────────────────────┘
```

If the job you want does not exist, does your company have plans to include such a position, or will you have to look for your ideal opportunity somewhere else?

```
┌─────────────────────────────────────────────────────────────┐
│                                                               │
│                                                               │
└─────────────────────────────────────────────────────────────┘
```

If the job you want is different from the job you have, what competencies or skills will you need for the future? Are they part of your continuous improvement and development plans? Do you currently have any of these competencies? How will you develop the necessary skills required to qualify for your ideal future job?

```
┌─────────────────────────────────────────────────────────────┐
│                                                               │
│                                                               │
└─────────────────────────────────────────────────────────────┘
```

What would the company gain from having you in that position? What is the basis for requesting the new job? How will you sell yourself to those who will decide?

```
┌─────────────────────────────────────────────────────────────┐
│                                                               │
│                                                               │
└─────────────────────────────────────────────────────────────┘
```

How realistic is it that you will get the position you want in your current company? Can you get ready for a future job and still do exceptional work in your current position?

- Is there a specific position in your company that could give you the opportunity to do what you want to be doing? Are you already in that job? Can your current job be modified to include some of the new things you would like to be doing?

- If the job you want does not exist, does your company have plans to include such a position, or will you have to look for your ideal opportunity somewhere else?

- If the job you want is different from the job you have, what competencies or skills will you need for the future? Are they part of your continuous improvement and development plans? Do you currently have any of these competencies? How will you develop the necessary skills required to qualify for your ideal future job?

- Are there many people interested in the job you want? How serious is the competition? What have you done so far to make sure the right people know that you are interested in the position? Is there anything else you need to do?

- How can you convince others, especially key decision makers, that you can do this other job well?

- What would the company gain from having you in that position? What is the basis for requesting the new job? How will you sell yourself to those who will decide?

- How realistic is it that you will get the position you want in your current company? Can you get ready for a future job and still do exceptional work in your current position?

Next, list some things you can do to stay informed about what's going on in your company, industry, and profession. Divide this list into three separate sections.

1. To stay informed about your company:

- Read annual reports, marketing brochures, sales forecasts, new product guides, company historical booklets, profiles of key employees, newsletters, and any other documents you can find to broaden your knowledge base.
- Volunteer for special project teams, especially those that will help you develop new skills, meet new people, and not interfere with your current performance. Go to meetings with an open mind and listen to what others have to say. Contribute your ideas and participate enthusiastically.

- Schedule informal coffee-break and lunch-time meetings with people in your Circle of Influence. Use these "touch base" times to share information about what is going on in the company and to discuss any areas of concern.
- Schedule short formal meetings with your manager for updates. Keep your manager informed about real or anticipated problems so that there are no surprises. Ask your manager for feedback about your performance and anything you should know about what is going on in the company that could help you meet your goals and priorities.

Tina Hartwell offers her ideas for staying up-to-date:

I always make sure I have a mentor. I established more formal relationships with people who can give me a different perspective about management issues and what's going on in the company. I track them down and spend time with them monthly. The people I have asked have told me they feel flattered and excited. Some have said, "We can learn from you, too," and we have developed very positive personal relationships. So don't be afraid to ask for help from someone you do not report to, someone who can help you learn. It's also important to network proactively outside your company. Build a portfolio of what skills you have, what you have done, what you can do, and who you know.

I feel that the key skills for people to master are problem-solving and analytical thinking. In companies where constant reorganization occurs, it will be important for people to be proactive and flexible.

Celestine Mack takes a proactive approach to conflict:

I don't wait for help or for someone to say, "Here's where you should go." I take control of my own destiny. I network, learn as much as I can, look for new challenges, try to find something I can grow into, and keep believing I can do anything I want to do.

2. To stay informed about your industry:

- Read current magazines about trends and new developments in your profession. Focus on books and periodicals that approach topics of importance to you on a level you can understand and apply immediately.

- Join industry associations and attend meetings that provide contact with others who do what you do for a living. Pay particular attention to what they have to say about trends or isolated incidents that are affecting their business.
- Be prepared to discuss common problems and to share your ideas about options and possible solutions.
- Get as competent as you can in the latest technology in your industry. Talk to experts about the best way to keep on top of changes and state-of-the-art processes.

Karen DiNunzio believes that becoming a life-long learner will help people succeed at work:

We need to value learning. Taking courses, volunteering for task forces to develop a broader range of skills, becoming more knowledgeable about technical skills—any activity that helps us learn something new can be beneficial. We need to learn as much as we can both at work and outside of work. Learning new things builds our brains so that our minds can handle different types of information and apply what we have learned to our changing work situations.

3. To stay informed about your profession:

- Read anything you can find about your profession, but be especially aware of articles and books that connect what you do with other businesses. If you are in a high-tech profession, for example, news stories about how computers are being used in physical therapy may present an idea about a future work possibility you may not have considered.
- Join professional organizations dedicated to identifying and resolving problems within your business. Begin with a local chapter and see if it meets your needs. You can always broaden your perspective later by joining a regional or national organization.
- Keep a list or a business card file of people you have met and gotten permission to call if you need to brainstorm. After your initial meeting, write a brief note on the back of the person's card about why you would need or want to stay in touch. The best networkers plant many seeds before they worry about cultivating any of them. Time then tells them which relationships might be most fruitful.

- If you have a piece of news someone on your list should know about, call and share the information. This will strengthen your relationship and help ensure that the connection is mutually beneficial.
- Do not overlook the strong connections you can build by participating in alumni associations, community groups like the Jaycees, civic volunteer work like the United Way, other local nonprofit organizations, or even a neighborhood fund-raising effort.
- Find advocates and sponsors in your organization who are willing to help you with your career. Of course, your manager should play an active role coaching and developing you. But remember to build connections with others who can support your good ideas, speak out for you when opportunities arise, and offer you direction about what you need to do to succeed or advance in your company. Cultivate your network of contacts in such a way that several people are on your side and willing to go to bat for you when the time comes.
- Take calculated risks with your career. Accept new challenges that you are ready (or at least nearly ready) to tackle. Know which assignments or opportunities have the greatest potential for failure.
- Keep track of your own accomplishments and successes. Develop a file that documents your contributions to your company's goals. Use objective language to describe what you have done: "Finished the Magellan project three weeks ahead of schedule"—"Designed a quality control process that will save our department $7,500 per year"—"Resolved a customer's complaint successfully and saved their $100,000 annual contract." This information may be important when you apply for a promotion within your company or develop a resume for a new job somewhere else.
- Know your internal competition and be honest about your chances to get ahead. With today's downsizing and reengineering activities, there are fewer advancement opportunities and more individuals lining up to get them. In today's fast-paced work environment, upward mobility may not be as good as lateral mobility. A lateral move, for example, might expand your skills, give you a broader base of experience for future opportunities, and provide you with more interesting challenges than you might get with a promotion. There may also be fewer headaches and pressures. Some individuals have actually taken a step or two backward to sharpen certain sales or computer skills to help improve their chances for longer-term advancement.

Elena Rubiales believes that up-to-date computer skills are absolutely essential:

Few people realize the potential of the software they use everyday. Most people learn the bare minimum to get by—enduring a computer rather than exploiting it. Good computer skills will set you apart.

The challenge is to stay as career-competitive as you can with others in your company. Your objective is to know what you want to do next and be ready when the opportunity comes along. Remember that unless you are self-employed, you are working with others and potentially competing with them for available opportunities.

The important thing to remember is that today there are a greater number of work options available in our global economy. There are many smaller companies that provide opportunities once available only in large corporations. Successful entrepreneurial ventures are more common than ever before, and people are finding creative ways to make their work a more meaningful part of their lives.

❖   ❖   ❖   ❖   ❖

CASE STUDY

Twenty years ago, Tom S. was a truck driver for a midsize medical supply company. Part of his work included learning the inventory, placing orders, and bringing special equipment into the homes of patients. During that time, Tom's company was purchased several times, and he actually worked at the same address for three different companies. He moved into the service department and immediately established a reputation for being conscientious, thorough, and caring. His good work did not go unnoticed, and he was made store manager of one of the company's biggest branches. There was a lot of pressure and many challenges associated with being a new supervisor, but Tom persevered. In fact, because of his understanding of his patients' needs and the types of equipment available, Tom developed a special rehab department that focused on sitting and mobility problems. The program is so successful that Tom travels around the country as the company's representative.

While Tom was managing his health care career, his sister, Mary, was a popular supervisor at a local Federal Credit Union. Her customers appreciated her courteous and warm style and often commented that Mary was always upbeat and pleasant. For the most part, the description was an accurate one. However, what people saw on the outside was not what Mary was feeling on the inside. She was in turmoil about her job. She did not completely understand her manager's expectations. Although they talked often, there were regular miscommunication problems. Mary also had a difficult time delegating and often took on tasks that others could have done. Her job kept getting bigger and her life busier. She realized she needed to make a change. She stayed for a few more years trying to make the best of the situation, but she finally decided to leave. She and her husband bought a small news store near their home and went into business for themselves.

Your Analysis

Before you read some of the reasons for these two different career decisions, take a few minutes to think about what you would have done in these situations.

_____

_____

_____

The Employee's Actions

In Tom's own words, there were three main reasons he stayed where he was even though the owners changed and new pressures built up:

- I always liked what I was doing, and I still do.
- I enjoy helping other people.
- I feel that I am good at what I do and people appreciate my efforts.

Today, Tom has two other reasons he is glad he stayed:

- I really like my manager.
- I feel as though I work for a company that is going to have an incredible impact on the health care industry.

In Mary's own words, there were several reasons for her difficult decision to leave:

- I always liked the people I worked with, and my customers were wonderful. But I just could not get the right balance between being helpful and doing everything myself.
- Whenever I thought about leaving, I got sad about missing the people and worried about losing my income. I was in the nineteenth year of a successful career that no longer made me happy. Security was important, but so was my sanity. I needed to find some new exciting challenge, and my very supportive husband helped us find exactly what we needed.

❖ ❖ ❖ ❖ ❖

When you review your current level of job satisfaction, make sure it is consistent with your overall sense of purpose. Are the demands and challenges of your work providing adequate financial and psychological rewards? Are you still having fun doing what you are being paid to do? Do you look forward to going to work each day because you enjoy your job and the people you work with? Figure 10-3 lists some factors that can

Figure 10-3. Evaluating your current level of job satisfaction.

	Yes	Most of the time	No
I like the people I am working with.			
The work I do is challenging.			
My manager gives me some freedom to operate independently.			
I often get new and exciting projects.			
I am encouraged to meet with people from other departments.			
I feel my contribution is valued by my manager and other executives.			

help you evaluate your current level of job satisfaction. If things seem out of balance, revise your plans to shift direction, accelerate your progress, or negotiate for a different alternative.

Always have a clear idea about the jobs and career paths that are available to you within your company, your industry, your profession. Keep an updated list of possible employers, interested headhunters, and contacts at two or three of your company's main competitors. Remember that an important part of this activity is increasing your professional value to your current employer or your next one.

Increasing Your Professional Value

- Hold yourself accountable for your own job performance. Set high personal standards and meet or beat them.
- Manage your own attitude, morale, motivation, and work habits. When you do a good job, be proud of your accomplishment, whether or not it is acknowledged by others.
- Share your success with those people who really matter to you. When you know you can do better, do better.
- Know what is important to you and consider these motivators whenever you evaluate your current level of job satisfaction. Check off any that are not being provided or are not meeting your needs:

Factors

Power_____ Control_____ Authority_____ Influence_____

Respect_____ Recognition_____ Praise_____ Awards_____

Status_____ Money_____ Promotion_____ New Title_____

Teamwork_____ Affiliation_____ Trust_____ Friendship_____

New Projects_____ Time off_____ Elimination of Routine Work_____

Relationships_____ Challenging Work_____ Other_____

Avoid falling into the trap of depending on others to manage your work, your development, and your career. In some cases, they are too busy. In other cases, what they want for themselves or for you may not be what you want. Ask for help, but stay in charge of your own work life. The more control you have over your own continuous improvement, your own professional development, and your own job performance, the easier it will be for you to make regular mid-career tune-ups and be successful and satisfied with your job.

11

Conclusion: Your Career Maintenance Schedule

The secret of joy in work is contained in the word excellence: To know how to do something well is to enjoy it.

—Pearl S. Buck, American novelist

As you come to the end of the book, we hope some of the ideas and techniques included here have helped you gain a new perspective on your current career.

If you have decided to stay in your present job and make it better than it has been, we will give you a few suggestions on how to do that. If you have decided that this is no longer the job that you want and it's time for you to move on, we will make some recommendations about that, too.

The first thing you need to do—and you probably have been doing this as you have been reading this book—is to make sure you have clarified your personal and professional expectations, needs, and interests. Determine what you expect from your job. Understand what motivates you. Is it money, power, affiliation, achievement, personal growth, a comfortable environment, or perhaps prestige?

Remember, also, that what motivated you in the past may no longer be your driving force. You may once have been motivated by money, status, or the opportunity for advancement. Now, however, job security may be your most important issue. So you may often need to reevaluate those forces behind what makes you do a good job. If you have decided to stay in your present job, you may need to make some changes to make it better, different, and filled with new approaches and exciting opportunities. Make sure your expectations are realistic, challenging, and achievable. Then put your work into a healthy perspective. Ask yourself these questions:

- Do you know what you want to be doing a year from now?
- Do you have a plan for moving along the path you would most like to take?
- Do you know what you want to be doing three to five years from now?
- How does your present job fit into that plan?
- Does your job provide the satisfaction you want? Does it meet your present and future needs?

As you conclude the book, we encourage you to review your expectations about what you are entitled to expect from your company. Regardless of your decision, in this final chapter, we will present some self-assessment tools for you to measure your skills and your readiness to either stay or make the changes you are contemplating. We will give you an opportunity to focus on a variety of self-evaluation forms.

You have a right to expect certain things from your company—to receive fair pay for a fair day's work, a safe environment to work in, equal opportunity, and the right to be treated with dignity. However, as organizations change, speed up, and put a greater emphasis on results, their expectations of you can undergo radical changes. Loyalty is no longer an important concept in American business. You may now be expected to do much more with fewer resources. What might have been a negotiable situation in the past may no longer be open for discussion. It is nobody's fault. It is just a fact of organizational life that everyone needs to accept.

The challenge for you now will be to determine how much room there is for give-and-take about performance issues you never have had to worry about in the past.

One way to maintain an open dialogue with others about your performance and priorities is to do periodic self-assessments. For example, if you find that one of the areas you need to improve is setting goals and priorities, the self-evaluation form in Figure 11-1 can provide useful information about changes and your response to them.

Use the form in Figure 11-2 to review any changes in the content and volume of your work.

Figure 11-3 contains a communication skills self-evaluation.

Update your Circle of Influence periodically to make sure it reflects any changes that may have occurred in the company, or in the list of contacts you need to succeed. Make certain you are keeping in touch with the right people on a regular basis. Use Figure 11-4 as a checklist for this.

(text continues on page 204)

Figure 11-1. Goal-setting and priorities self-evaluation.

Have your goals and priorities changed recently?

What caused the changes?

Were you able to anticipate the changes and deal with them effectively?

Do you anticipate additional changes?

What impact have the changes had on your overall performance?

Are you doing what your company is paying you to do, what your company needs you to do?

If there are any problems, what steps have you taken to correct them?

Are there specific individuals you need to spend more time with, or are there specific individuals you are spending too much time with?

Key learnings

Figure 11-2. Balancing multiple demands self-evaluation.

Have you experienced any changes in the content and volume of your work?

```
┌─────────────────────────────────────────────────────┐
│                                                       │
│                                                       │
└─────────────────────────────────────────────────────┘
```

When changes have occurred, what adjustments have you made?

```
┌─────────────────────────────────────────────────────┐
│                                                       │
│                                                       │
└─────────────────────────────────────────────────────┘
```

Have you needed help from others?

```
┌─────────────────────────────────────────────────────┐
│                                                       │
│                                                       │
└─────────────────────────────────────────────────────┘
```

If there has been any resistance from others, how have you dealt with it?

```
┌─────────────────────────────────────────────────────┐
│                                                       │
│                                                       │
└─────────────────────────────────────────────────────┘
```

Do you feel you have control of your time? If not, what adjustments do you need to make?

```
┌─────────────────────────────────────────────────────┐
│                                                       │
│                                                       │
└─────────────────────────────────────────────────────┘
```

Have you overcome your major time wasters? Are you assertive with people who tend to take advantage of your time?

```
┌─────────────────────────────────────────────────────┐
│                                                       │
│                                                       │
└─────────────────────────────────────────────────────┘
```

Are there any special skills or techniques you are using now that you want to make sure you remember for the future?

```
┌─────────────────────────────────────────────────────┐
│                                                       │
│                                                       │
└─────────────────────────────────────────────────────┘
```

Key learnings

```
┌─────────────────────────────────────────────────────┐
│                                                       │
│                                                       │
│                                                       │
└─────────────────────────────────────────────────────┘
```

Figure 11-3. Communication skills self-evaluation.

Remember that your reputation depends on your willingness to share information that will help others to succeed.

	Yes, I am always truthful	*I am guilty of convenient credibility*	*If the truth puts me in a bad light I avoid it*
Have you withheld information for you own benefit when you knew that information would help others?			
Have you felt that others withheld information from you?			
What steps have you taken to correct this?			
Do you always tell the truth?			
How would you describe your current level of credibility?			
Do other people consider you trustworthy?			
Do others know they can count on you to be truthful with them?			

Once you have completed a few of these self-evaluation forms, see if there are any patterns or trends that need your immediate attention.

Are there important communication problems that need your immediate attention?

Are there certain performance factors that you want to make sure you repeat?

Key learnings

Figure 11-4. Developing productive relationships self-evaluation.

Take a close look at your Circle Of Influence to be sure the right people are in your support group. Focus on one person at a time and ask yourself how you are doing in your communication efforts with each person.

Are you giving them honest, accurate, and timely information?

Are you getting the same from them?

If there are any problems, what have you done to correct them?

Key learnings

Finally, establish and maintain a regular career maintenance schedule for yourself. The most successful career managers use a variety of simple checklists. They record their progress in a journal that they keep current. These may be nothing more than notes, brief suggestions to themselves, reminders, notes from meetings, or suggestions that key people have made to them. They also record important learnings from past experiences, areas for improvement, processes that worked well for them, obstacles they overcame, and names of people who came through when they needed help.

Remember that a mid-career tune-up is not a one-shot process. Most successful people review their careers several times a year even if they decide not to make a change. The self-assessment tools provided here will help you look at one, a few, or all key performance dimensions of your job. Use Figures 11-5 through 11-10 to focus on specific work habits that will keep you ahead of others in this fast-paced work world.

There is a classic story about a pilgrim walking through a medieval town in Europe. He saw a man at work and asked, "What work are you doing?" The man continued his work and said, "I am chipping stone." The pilgrim walked on and came upon a second man doing exactly the same task and asked him, "What work are you doing?" The worker looked at him and said, "I am carving a column." The pilgrim continued on his journey until he met a third man doing exactly the same work as the previous two men. Again, the pilgrim asked, "What work are you doing?" The third man smiled proudly and answered, "I am building a Cathedral."

Each craftsman had exactly the same job. What they were doing was actually less important than their perception of its value and importance. Even the most mundane and routine tasks can take on increased significance if you make up your mind that your work is making a difference to someone. Look around at the people inside and outside of your company who benefit from what you do. Are you making life better for your external customers? Are you making life easier for one of your coworkers? Have you taken pressure off your manager by accepting more responsibility or resolving problems more independently? Asking yourself these types of questions will help you gain a new perspective about the real contributions you are making and about the kind of foundation you are building at work.

Figure 11-5. Conflict resolution self-evaluation.

Describe the last interpersonal conflict you had with someone at work.

What were the key factors that created it?

What made you decide to confront it?

How did you describe the value of resolving the conflict in your conversation with the other person?

What the conflict successfully resolved? What did you do to ensure its successful resolution?

Key learnings

Figure 11-6. Fix your own problems self-evaluation.

Describe a recent situation in which you resolved a problem on your own.

```



```

List a few of the techniques you used, especially any you want to re-member to use again.

```



```

Were there any techniques you tried that did not work as well as you wanted them to?

```



```

Key learnings

```



```

Figure 11-7. Creativity self-evaluation.

List as many creative, flexible, innovative approaches you have tried in the past month.

Which techniques worked?

Which would you try again?

Which would you recommend to others?

Key learnings

Figure 11-8. Adapting to change self-evaluation.

What is the most significant change in your work area in the past three months?

```
┌─────────────────────────────────────────────────────────┐
│                                                           │
│                                                           │
└─────────────────────────────────────────────────────────┘
```

Were you ready for it?

```
┌─────────────────────────────────────────────────────────┐
│                                                           │
│                                                           │
└─────────────────────────────────────────────────────────┘
```

What did you do to prepare yourself and how did you manage to change?

```
┌─────────────────────────────────────────────────────────┐
│                                                           │
│                                                           │
└─────────────────────────────────────────────────────────┘
```

Were you reluctant to make this change at first?

```
┌─────────────────────────────────────────────────────────┐
│                                                           │
│                                                           │
└─────────────────────────────────────────────────────────┘
```

What factors made the change easier for you?

```
┌─────────────────────────────────────────────────────────┐
│                                                           │
│                                                           │
└─────────────────────────────────────────────────────────┘
```

How did you deal with your own resistance and that of other people?

```
┌─────────────────────────────────────────────────────────┐
│                                                           │
│                                                           │
└─────────────────────────────────────────────────────────┘
```

How would you describe the main driving forces?

```
┌─────────────────────────────────────────────────────────┐
│                                                           │
│                                                           │
└─────────────────────────────────────────────────────────┘
```

What would you do differently next time?

```
┌─────────────────────────────────────────────────────────┐
│                                                           │
│                                                           │
└─────────────────────────────────────────────────────────┘
```

Key learnings

```
┌─────────────────────────────────────────────────────────┐
│                                                           │
│                                                           │
└─────────────────────────────────────────────────────────┘
```

Figure 11-9. Managing morale self-evaluation.

Describe a time in the last month when your morale was lower than usual.

```
[                                                                    ]
```

What caused it?

```
[                                                                    ]
```

What did you do to improve?

```
[                                                                    ]
```

Did you do this on your own or did you depend on someone else to help you?

```
[                                                                    ]
```

Figure 11-10. Career maintenance checklist.

What projects have I handled well since my last maintenance check?

```
┌─────────────────────────────────────────────────────────────┐
│                                                               │
│                                                               │
│                                                               │
└─────────────────────────────────────────────────────────────┘
```

What skills did I contribute that made this a success?

```
┌─────────────────────────────────────────────────────────────┐
│                                                               │
│                                                               │
│                                                               │
└─────────────────────────────────────────────────────────────┘
```

Who helped me be a success at this project?

```
┌─────────────────────────────────────────────────────────────┐
│                                                               │
│                                                               │
│                                                               │
└─────────────────────────────────────────────────────────────┘
```

How did they help?

```
┌─────────────────────────────────────────────────────────────┐
│                                                               │
│                                                               │
│                                                               │
└─────────────────────────────────────────────────────────────┘
```

Have there been projects that were less than successful because of skills I lacked?

```
┌─────────────────────────────────────────────────────────────┐
│                                                               │
│                                                               │
│                                                               │
└─────────────────────────────────────────────────────────────┘
```

What steps have I made toward developing these skills?

```
┌─────────────────────────────────────────────────────────────┐
│                                                               │
│                                                               │
│                                                               │
└─────────────────────────────────────────────────────────────┘
```

Are there specific performance areas that I need to improve? What types of projects cause me the most difficulties? Are there performance areas I need to focus on to improve the way I deal with those specific projects?

```
┌─────────────────────────────────────────────────────────────┐
│                                                               │
│                                                               │
│                                                               │
└─────────────────────────────────────────────────────────────┘
```

Key learnings

```
┌─────────────────────────────────────────────────────────────┐
│                                                               │
│                                                               │
│                                                               │
└─────────────────────────────────────────────────────────────┘
```

Index